PRAYING WITH OUR EYES OPEN

PRAYING WITH OUR EYES OPEN

ENGENDERING FEMINIST LITURGICAL PRAYER

Marjorie Procter-Smith

ABINGDON PRESS
Nashville

PRAYING WITH OUR EYES OPEN

Copyright © 1995 by Abingdon Press

Library of Congress Cataloging-in-Publication Data

Procter-Smith, Marjorie
    Praying with our eyes open : engendering feminist liturgical prayer / Marjorie Procter-Smith.
        p.   cm.
    Includes bibliographical references and index.
    ISBN 0-687-39122-9 (pbk. : alk paper)
    1. Prayer—Christianity.   2. Liturgics.   3. Feminist theology.
    4. Feminism—Religious aspects—Christianity.   5. Sexism in liturgical language.
    I. Title.
    BV226.P74   1995
    264' .0082—dc20
                                                                    95-38861
                                                                    CIP

Scripture quotations, unless otherwise noted, are from The New Revised Standard Version Bible, copyright © 1989 by the Division of Christian Education of the National Council of Churches of Christ in the USA. Used by permission.

The excerpt from the poem "Artemis," taken from *Beginning with O* by Olga Broumas (New Haven: Yale University Press, 1977), copyright © Yale University Press, is used by permission.

The excerpt from the poem "Unlearning not to speak," by Marge Piercy, *Circles on the Water*, Alfred A. Knopf, copyright © 1971, 1980 by Marge Piercy and Middlemarsh, Inc., is used by permission of The Wallace Literary Agency, Inc. and Alfred A. Knopf, Inc.

The text of the chant for "Blessing over Milk and Honey," from the Re-imagining Program Booklet, 1993, is used by kind permission of the Rev. Dr. Hilda Kuester.

Verse and refrain from "Victory in Jesus," by E. M. Bartlett/Albert E. Brumley and Sons/SESAC. Used by permission.

The prayer, "O God whose word is life," by Janet Morley, copyright © 1988, 1992 by Janet Morley is reprinted by permission of Morehouse Publishing (North American rights) from the book by Janet Morley, *All Desires Known: Inclusive Prayers for Worship and Meditation*, p. 9, originally published by SPCK. Other English-language world rights by SPCK. Used by permission of the publisher.

95 96 97 98 99 00 01 02 03 04—10 9 8 7 6 5 4 3 2 1

MANUFACTURED IN THE UNITED STATES OF AMERICA

For my women friends
from whom I have learned
resistance
courage
hope
and love
and for whom I am truly thankful

CONTENTS

SEARCHING FOR THE WORD FOR FIRE

I am a woman committed to
a politics
of transliteration, the methodology

of a mind
stunned at the suddenly
possible shifts of meaning—for which
like amnesiacs

in a ward on fire, we must
find words
or burn

Olga Broumas, "Artemis"[1]

This is a book about prayer for women who don't—or can't—pray, written by a woman who often has difficulty praying. Most books on prayer are written on the assumption that the reader prays, or wants to pray, that the act of prayer itself is not problematic, only we humans are problematic. Prayer is presented as a good, desirable, and for the Christian, necessary part of one's spiritual life. Prayer, in this way of thinking, may be deeply personal or sublimely communal, but it is never seen as political.

This book begins with the assertion that traditional Christian public prayer (and, by extension, private and personal prayer) is based on problematic assumptions about the nature of God, about the nature of human life and need, about the necessary rituals which surround the act of prayer. This book also insists that prayer is a profoundly political act. That is, prayer, especially public prayer, engages the participants in a web of interlocking assumptions about bodies, communities, God, Jesus (in Christian prayer), human nature, the world, and relationships. Furthermore, the assumptions set in place and maintained by public prayer do not take place in a vacuum, but in the public arena, an arena marked by racism, sexism, heterosexism, classism, and other forms of interlocking oppressions and subjugations. In this context, Christian prayer, both in form and content, often serves to reinforce and spiritualize multiple forms of oppression.

The beginnings of this book are many. Initially I was intrigued by the apparent absence of corporate prayer in feminist liturgical gatherings. These gatherings were predominantly Christian, predominantly Protestant, made up of women who, for the most part, were engaged in worship traditions that valued prayer highly, especially pastoral prayer. Yet in feminist gatherings, both in classroom settings and in more voluntary gatherings, prayers in the conventional sense seemed to be absent. I say "apparent absence," and "seemed to be absent," because some participants/ planners, when asked about this absence, insisted that prayer was present. But it was (in my view, at least) certainly not prayer in any conventional Protestant sense. That is, it was not primarily verbal discourse using the recognizable rhetorical devices of Protestant address to God. This raised for me the interesting question of why this conventional form had been rejected in favor of more diffuse and nonverbal forms, replacing meditation and contemplation, so to speak, for prayer.

Yet, while I was noting and considering these questions, I also began to hear other voices, women's voices, expressing reluctance or inability to pray. These voices were those of women survivors of male violence and abuse of all sorts, and of those who cared about them and knew the stories of abuse. In the face of terrible suffering, suffering that the church failed to recognize in its prayer and justified in its teachings about the place of women and the power of men, these women found themselves unable or unwilling to pray. One woman, an adult survivor of incest, spoke of the necessity of silence in her recovery process. During her process of recovery of memory of incest, she reported that she was unable to pray; she was numb, spiritually as well as emotionally. What she needed was both the permission not to pray and the knowledge that those who were able were praying for her. Because of the traditional Christian use of male-identified language to speak to God, survivors of male violence find themselves questioning whether God is trustworthy.

And I myself began to experience doubts about the perennial appropriateness of prayer. A woman survivor of family violence asked me to help her plan a healing service for herself. She was more than capable of designing a ritual to answer to her needs; she asked me to offer only a closing prayer. In turning to conventional models of Christian prayer, I found myself unable to claim anything in this tradition of confession, thanksgiving, and petition that seemed appropriate to the occasion. Certainly there was much to confess in this woman's life, but not on her part or on the part of anyone of the small group of close friends who would be present; certainly all of us there could and did give ample thanks for the courageous and creative woman for whom the ritual was held; and petitions for her continued well-being were in all our hearts. But the conventions failed miserably to acknowledge her—and our—anger and outrage at the wholly unnecessary suffering inflicted on her, not only by her father, but also by the church that ignored her suffering and denied his violent behavior. And where was God when she was being beaten? What needed to be said to God could not be fitted into the form of traditional Christian prayer. Finally, I turned to Jewish prayer forms as having a more developed sense of lament and anger. But the questions this task raised stayed with me, making me continually uncomfortable with most Christian prayer.

The human attempt to find the right words for prayer, the means of addressing the holy, often has the desperate urgency described by the poet Olga Broumas. We are searching for the word for fire, in a burning room. Jacob wrestles with the angel. Paul acknowledges the struggle: "Likewise the Spirit helps us in our weakness; for we do not know how to pray as we ought, but the Spirit [her]self intercedes for us with sighs too deep for words" (Romans 8:26). Human attempts to address the Holy One are not only urgent, Paul suggests, but also flawed.

It is both these facts—the urgency and the flaw—that fuel this work. Feminists indeed acknowledge that the church "does not know how to pray as it ought." And feminists of biblical faith are women "committed to a politics of transliteration," "amnesiacs in a ward on fire," knowing that the shifts of meaning we are seeing, the shifts of meaning that we are bringing about, mean that we must "find words or burn."

And it is both the urgency and the flaw which lead to the

feminist prayer posture suggested in the title of the book. Praying with our eyes open suggests that we are conscious of the risks of our position as feminists in biblical religion. The mood of the Christian churches at this writing is one of threat to feminists and others who wish to see the church open itself to the gifts of women of all races, abilities, and sexual orientation; to gay persons, to the poor, to the oppressed. In times of persecution, it is advisable not to close one's eyes to one's own personal risk or to what is going on around us. Yet we pray, at times, seeking new ways of addressing our deepest desires to the Holy One, even as we doubt the beneficence or power of the One we address.

But this is not a study concerned primarily with private, personal prayer. Women and other disenfranchised groups within the church have always been able to claim the margins of Christian prayer in the realm of the private, the internal, the domestic. Indeed, patriarchal church strictures have actively encouraged women to develop their particular form of prayer in private, as an appropriate form of "feminine spirituality." In some ways, the development of feminist prayer and spirituality groups replicates the patriarchal dichotomy that assigns women to the private sphere. Until the Re-Imagining Conference in Minneapolis in November of 1994, malestream church leaders were content to "allow" women to have their spirituality groups, since they had little or no impact on public practice. Certainly the conference provided a convenient scapegoat for disgruntled retrogressive elements within malestream Protestantism; but much of the outrage generated by these groups focused on the public prayer for the event.

In particular, the "Milk and Honey" ritual was interpreted as a substitute for, and therefore in some sense a revision of, the Christian eucharist. More than anything else, it was this perceived movement from the margins to the center of Christian prayer that enraged retrogressive religious groups. Some planners of the event have argued, in response to the attacks and charges of heresy, that the ritual was not intended as a eucharist. However, I would argue that women need to claim the center of Christian public prayer, to disrupt and construct, deliberately and intentionally, central, defining Christian public prayer. Why not understand the Milk and Honey ritual as a eucharist? Whose interests are protected in controlling the content and meaning of Christian eucharistic praying?

I agree with Elisabeth Schüssler Fiorenza's proposal of the image of the feminist theologian as "troublemaker, as a resident alien, who constantly seeks to destabilize the centers, both the value-free, ostensibly neutral research ethos of the academy and the dogmatic authoritarian stance of patriarchal religion."[2] Women have long been defined as marginal to the production of scientific and theological knowledge, as Schüssler Fiorenza observes. But we also have been defined as marginal to the creation of liturgical and ritual language. Therefore we must disrupt these processes of marginalization, claim the central prayers of the church as our prayers, and thereby transform them from the language of the rulers to the language of the whole free people of God.

I had at first thought to call this book by the rather pessimistic title, "Without a Prayer." Not only did many feminist liturgies appear prayer-less, it was not clear to me that there was any reason for feminist groups to engage in prayer, at least by traditional definitions of the practice. Have women not always prayed—for deliverance from violence and abuse, for protection for our children, for survival, for peace and well-being? And have we not continued to know violence and abuse, destruction or damage of our children, loss and death and silence? Prayer to an allegedly almighty Father-God seemed worse than pointless; it seemed an insult added to the generations of injury suffered by women. Yet a different kind of prayer is emerging in feminist liturgy groups, among those marginalized by the powerful in the religious communities. These forms and styles of prayer, discussed and exampled here, are not just signs of hope (to name oneself feminist is to hope), but the very stuff of hope. They are starters of hope, as sourdough starter is the basis for bread: full of life and energy, capable of multiplying themselves and carrying their energy forward into countless loaves, beautiful and diverse.

This book might be well understood as a book of recipes. Recipe-knowledge is often discredited as being mere repetition of something created by others, or unimaginative and pedestrian measurements and timing, creativity measured in teaspoons and degrees Fahrenheit. But I prefer to think of recipe knowledge as a kind of alchemy, the almost magical transformation of unlikely substances into nourishment and health. Cooking requires strate-

.gies. So does feminist prayer. And finally, strategy is what I am concerned about in this book. Some theological strategies are harmful, unhealthy. Some prayer strategies are dangerous to the well-being of women. And some strategies are useful for survival, but not for thriving.

Strategy presumes an objective, a goal. What are the objectives of feminist liturgical prayer? I have already suggested that women's well-being and spiritual health is one objective. But what does such well-being and health look like? Living as we do in a culture and a time deeply marked by hatred and fear of women, how do we reimagine the world and the church with women's well-being at the heart? Another objective has also been mentioned: claiming the center of the churches' life and work, particularly its ritual life and work. But again one must ask, the center of what church, or what kind of church? If the church in its present state is what we aspire to, we can only accept the empty, hierarchical center, devoted to the repression of difference and change.

So I conclude that the goal of feminist liturgical prayer is resistance and transformation. Resistance to patterns of domination, not only domination of women by men, but also domination of women by women. Awareness of how these relationships of domination function is essential to the creation of prayers of resistance, prayers that spiritualize sociability, cooperation, and mutuality rather than dominance and submission. And transformation because this is the reason for the resistance to dominance. We resist in order to transform, to recreate the church as communal, sociable, healthy.

This book is definitely written from a Christian perspective, although some readers may find my form of Christianity strange, or objectionable, or even non-Christian. Yet Christianity is the religion that has chosen me, and for now at least it is the one I choose (even as I reject parts of it). I have long been interested in the different ways that Jewish feminists approach prayer, and find neopagan feminist ritual and prayer intriguing. Both of these practices influence the development of Christian feminist prayer to varying degrees. However, as I cannot claim identity as a Jew or a neopagan, I will limit myself in this book to consideration of Christian feminist problems and strategies. Whether these can be useful for others I cannot say.

14

This book is also written out of a growing awareness of the pervasiveness of violence and abuse in women's lives. Although I am fortunate enough not to have lived with imminent danger of physical or psychological violence, I no longer take such good fortune for granted. I now understand that the culture in which we live is deeply hostile to women's well-being; although I am shielded by race and class privilege from many of the overt hostilities, I know that my safety is always precarious. This self-awareness, together with what I have learned from reading the work of feminists writing on violence against women and (above all) from women who have trusted me with their stories of struggle and survival, has been pivotal for me. This knowledge has deeply influenced my understanding of Christian faith and practice, and it deeply influences the ideas and proposals presented in this book.

Many beautiful and diverse people served as "starters of hope" for this book. Beth Cooper supplied the title, and much inspiration, before even the conception of the project. She also served as my research assistant during the initial stages of research on the topic. Millie Feske provided hope and courage and no end of nourishing conversations in person and by way of "FE-mail." She also graciously provided typescripts of her excellent and provocative papers on a feminist critique of redemption, work that has been decisive in my own thinking on the subject. Carol Adams supplied missing quotations, useful references, and supportive critique and encouragement in equal measure. Her own work in feminist theory, especially on violence against women, has profoundly influenced my own work. Janet Walton read early drafts of portions the book, made valuable suggestions, and added necessary good strategic advice, as always. The members of the Feminist Liturgy Seminar of the North American Academy of Liturgy responded to early reports on this research. Danna Fewell, Diedre Palmer, Pat Davis, Marilyn Alexander, Janice Virtue, and Jouette Bassler listened to me gripe about the writing process and provided sisterly support and encouragement at low points. Diedre Palmer loaned me the book that contained the wonderful print that appears on the cover of this book.

I am grateful to Perkins School of Theology for a leave to do the initial research for this project, and to the Association of Theological Schools for a Research and Scholarship grant to support that leave during the academic year 1990–1991. The theology department of the University of Notre Dame invited me to give a lecture in the summer of 1994 which served as an opportunity to test some of these ideas on another audience. Ulrike Guthrie models the best example of editorial guidance and support; I feel extremely fortunate to be able to work with her. George, as ever, is faithful to the deepest meaning of this book. He engendered stimulating conversation on many of the ideas in here on the way to and from the barn, and graciously gave up time during his own leave to provide valuable copyediting on a tight schedule. Jeremy continues to live out his own courage and imagination in ways that astonish, delight, and humble me. Thanks are due, also, to the nonhumans who live with us: Howie, Susanna, Frost, Funnyface, the rabbits in all their multiplicity and individuality, and especially Annie and Copycat. They helped me keep a sense of proportion about this and all such transient and limited human projects.

PRAYING BETWEEN THE LINES
Unitary Prayer Language and the Necessity of Heteroglossia

Like desire, language disrupts, refuses to be contained within boundaries.

bell hooks, *Teaching to Transgress*[1]

What is feminist public prayer?[2] Is there such a thing? Will resolutions of questions about God-language resolve questions about feminist prayer? Or does the prayer language of the church reflect the weight of centuries of patriarchy and deep ambivalence about women's voice and presence before God? How do women claim their voice in address to God in public prayer?

These questions about prayer arise in the context of the feminist critique of Christian theology and practice in general, and in the more specific context of the feminist liturgical movement.[3] The feminist liturgical movement has evolved three layers of questions about the churches' liturgical practices.

The first question raised by the feminist liturgical movement is a question of *inclusion*: Are we included in the churches' proclamation and prayer *as women*? This question arose out of a dissatisfaction with the use of male-referenced language in liturgy and prayer. Although church representatives argued that the use of "man" for people and "He" for God included women by implication, feminists retorted that being included only by implication did not include them as women. The insistence on being included as women is embodied in the push for women to have access to ordination and appointment as religious liturgical leaders. Thus questions about inclusive language are tied to questions about inclusive leadership. These questions in turn lead to reexamination of the use of language in prayers, sermons, liturgical and biblical texts.[4] Women's access to ordained ministry and public liturgical presidency also raises questions about authority and power (do women wield it differently?) as well as preaching and presiding style, vesture, and use of nonverbal language.

The second question arises out of the first question of inclusion. If we are in fact included as women, then what is our story as women? Where are we in the Christian story? This is a question of *retrieval and recovery*. Rediscovery of women of the biblical and historical past requires reconception of lectionaries (are women's stories included?), sermons and bible studies, and this will lead to creation of liturgical and homiletical materials based on this recovery of history.

The third question arises out of this recovery, as the complexity of the history of women in Christianity becomes clearer. Women in Christian history are neither simply victims nor victors, but participants in, and at times resisters to, patriarchal society. This raises questions about adequacy and truth: Is it (any given doctrine, practice, or tradition) true for us as women? This last question has led the feminist liturgical movement beyond questions of inclusion and retrieval to questions of *transformation*. How can the Christian faith in general and its liturgies and prayers in specific be transformed into a feminist Christian faith? What are the resources for such transformation and what are the necessary strategies?

In many ways feminist questions about public prayer mirror other feminist questions about recognition and legitimation of women's public voice and presence. At stake, in large part, is the question of whether women have the right and power to speak. In the words of Carolyn Heilbrun, "Power is the ability to take one's place in whatever discourse is essential to action and the right to have one's part matter."[5] In addition to this question about women's power to speak, for the believing Christian feminist there is also the question of women's right and power to speak to God. Since public prayer is address to God on behalf of the worshiping community, women's representational power is also at stake. Can women legitimately address God directly in public on behalf of the whole community? Can women legitimately bring their concerns and needs as women to that encounter, and trust that they matter?

Ambivalence about women's power to speak to God in public and for others runs deep in the Christian prayer tradition. The reasons for this ambivalence include fear and antipathy toward the female body; assumptions of male domination and female subservience as divinely ordained and/or modeled; protocols of prayer adopted from imperial court protocols; the dichotomy between public and private; hierarchical male images and names for God; and the significance assigned to the maleness of Jesus. The problems of God and Jesus will be dealt with in later chapters. For now it is necessary first to consider the interpretive framework that supports ideas of male dominance and gender dichotomy, before turning to an examination of feminist forms of resistance to dichotomized prayer.

A Note on Prayer and Theology

In this book I will be making a distinction between prayer and theology: theology (or theological reflection) is primarily language *about* God; prayer is primarily language *with* (or to, or toward) God. Many liturgical theologians would not wish to draw so sharp a line between the two. Don Saliers, for example, argues that "prayer is a logically required context for the utterance of theological truths."[6] Saliers and others wish to correct what they view as an unfortunate split between the expressions of prayer and ritual on the one hand and the doing of systematic theology on the other.

I agree with the view that prayer and ritual are prior to, and form the context for, theological reflection. My point is somewhat different: it is about difference in language and tone. The language of theology, at least in Western Christendom, has been the language of reason, of logic, of philosophy. The language of prayer, however, even as it has been influenced by rather detached Greco-Roman legal language, remains the language of conversation, of encounter. Although in fact there seems to be no reason why a theologian couldn't write a conversational systematic theology, it hasn't been done. This is like the difference between conversation and dissertation. In any case, I do not regard this difference in tone as a problem at all, but simply as a recognition of the way things are. But what follows from this observation is that this consideration of prayer will not proceed as if it were a systematic theological treatment of prayer. Instead it will more nearly resemble prayer, in that it will be concerned primarily with relationship, and in particular the relationship between God and women who pray.

What kinds of relationship between God and those who pray are indicated by contemporary public prayer? What kinds of relationship are created and supported, what kinds are denied or rejected? Or, to put it more personally, Does God care about me, or pay attention to me? Where is God when massive preventable suffering is taking place? Because prayer takes place in the midst of questions such as these, it has an urgency that theological reflection doesn't have. We need suggestions, proposals, and strategies for responding to these questions now, and the problems must be worked out in the process of praying, of finding new ways to enter into conversation with God so that women's voices and languages are heard and acknowledged, both by the community and by God.

Traditional Prayer Language as a Unitary Language

In its public prayer, the church reiterates who it believes God to be, and what it believes our relationship is with that God. One might even argue that whatever the church knows about God, little as it is, it knows it as a direct result of the urgent fiery struggle for words to speak with the Holy One. The forms in which it has done this have varied, but the greatest variations have been allowed in the more private and less controlled arena of private and mystical prayer.

Public corporate prayer, in the Western Christian tradition, has drawn predominantly from the discourse and protocol of public language of the ancient Greco-Roman world. It has also drawn primarily from the prayer discourse of the powerful, which is privileged in the church's public prayer. Patriarchal discourse desires to establish and maintain power. In order to do this, it strives for a unified voice, for unitary discourse. But since reality is not one, but multiple, varied, and diverse, a dichotomous way of thinking is necessary to create a unitary discourse. Desire for unity is reflected in what Nancy Jay called "A, Not-A" thinking. This form of dichotomous thinking creates two absolute categories with nothing in common. It originates in Aristotle's development of principles of logic. The most basic of these are: the Principle of Identity (A), the Principle of Contradiction (Not-A), and the Principle of the Excluded Middle (everything must be either A or Not-A):

> In A/Not-A dichotomies only one term has positive reality; Not-A is only the privation or absence of A. . . . The structure of A/Not-A is such that a third term is impossible: everything and anything must be either A or Not-A. Such distinctions are all-encompassing. . . . This all-encompassing capacity is a consequence of a quality of Not-A called "the infinitation of the negative."[7]

As Jay observed, these are principles of pure logic, unexplainable by observation or experience of the real world, where everything is in a constant state of change. But they are principles often enforced in the real world, particularly in dichotomous religions, sometimes by the use or threat of violence.

She goes on to explain that this infinite quality of the Not-A side of the dichotomy is what makes it undefinable, thus uncontrollable, and therefore associated with chaos, pollution, and danger. In dichotomous religions, Jay argues, women are associated with Not-A, men with the pure, well-defined A. This logical insight helps understand such religious dichotomies as sacred/profane, male/female, public/private, and soul/body; it can usefully be applied to liturgical language as a form of discourse as well.

Christian religious discourse has tended to accept this form of dichotomous thinking, as Jay points out, even as it also includes within its tradition, uncomfortably, non-dichotomous thinking. The Christian preference for hierarchical dichotomies is found in many places. The *via negativa* tradition of defining God by saying what God is not employs the infinitation of the negative and thus preserves the inviolability and absolute otherness of God. But as ideas about God came under the influence of Platonic philosophic thought, God's unchanging nature became important to argue. Thus God was placed on the A side of the equation, since change is, of course, Not-A. Further, as Jay points out, this dichotomy provides the logical structure behind Levitical purity laws. Women are identified with the chaotic, dangerous, unlimited Not-A side in Christian thought as well as in Levitical law.[8]

Christian thought has been particularly dichotomous in its

thinking about its own identity. Christian/non-Christian, Christian/Jew, Christian/pagan, orthodox/heretic, and Catholic/Protestant are dichotomous categories that have become deeply embedded in Christian discourse. It is Christianity (or some particular form of it) which is A; all else is Not-A and therefore, as Jay puts it, "tends toward infinitation: impurity, irrationality, disorder, chaos, change, chance (the goddess Fortuna), error, and evil."[9]

Examples abound. The early Christian document called the *Didache* (dated, according to some scholars, around 90 C.E.) begins with a lengthy moral instruction known as "the Two Ways":

> There are two ways, one of life, and one of death; and between the
> two ways there is a great difference.[10]

In the case of the *Didache*, the dichotomy is a moral rather than theological one; the great difference between the two ways is marked by differences in behavior, not in acceptance of doctrines. The "way of death" is clearly identified with chaotic, disordered activities:

> But the way of death is this: First of all, it is wicked and thoroughly
> blasphemous: murders, adulteries, lusts, fornications, thefts, idola-
> tries, magic arts, sorceries, robberies, false witness, hypocrisies,
> duplicity, deceit, arrogance, malice, stubbornness, greediness,
> filthy talk, jealousy, audacity, haughtiness, boastfulness.[11]

These behaviors have to do with violation of boundaries: sexual (fornication, lust, adultery), material (murder, theft, robbery, greed), social (false witness, hypocrisy and duplicity, boastfulness, etc.), or religious (idolatries, magic arts, sorcery). Thus the "way of life" respects and observes proper boundaries; the "way of death" violates them.

Another form of dichotomous thinking is reflected in the sermon of Melito of Sardis, a second-century bishop, who sharply contrasts Judaism/Israel with Christianity/Church, in order to emphasize not only the superiority of Christianity, but also its role as replacement for Judaism. It is unthinkable for Melito that Christianity and Judaism might co-exist. Because they are oppositional, one must give way to the other; according to Melito's logic, the old must give way to the new. Christianity is A; Judaism is Not-A; in order to protect the purity of Christianity, it must be distinguished from Judaism as sharply as possible:

> The model was precious before the reality, the parable splendid before its fulfillment. That is to say, the people was precious before the Church was established, the Law was marvelous before the Gospel shed its light. But when the Church was established and the Gospel proclaimed, the figure was found wanting as its image had changed to reality. The Law was at an end as it had transmitted its strength to the Gospel. Just so, the figure becomes bankrupt when it transmits its image to reality, and the parable is bankrupt when it is clarified by interpretation. So also the Law was terminated when the Gospel came to light, and the people lost identity when the Church took its place. And the figure was abolished when the Lord became manifest and what was precious yesterday is today regarded as useless, because what is truly precious has appeared.[12]

Melito's "replacement theology" provides another form of dichotomous thinking, in which "Not-A" (in this case, Judaism) is not simply chaotic and dangerous, but it ceases to exist in any meaningful way: it "loses identity" and becomes "useless." This loss of identity and uselessness, in Melito's interpretation, is dramatized by Melito's blame of Jews for the death of Jesus, and God's corresponding rejection of the Jews:

> You have abandoned the Lord, and have not found pity with him; you have destroyed the Lord, and you lie pulverized in turn. You lie prostrate, a corpse, while he has risen from the dead, and has ascended to the highest heavens.[13]

In this chilling text, the horrifying possibilities of dichotomous logic are manifested. In anti-Jewish as well as anti-heretical writings, Christian leaders placed dichotomous logic at the service of dichotomizing strategies. Christian identity was established at the expense of difference and diversity. The anti-heretical writings of Irenaeus, second-century bishop of Lyons, are representative of the dichotomizing strategy common in the church of this period:

> Certain men, rejecting the truth, are introducing among us false stories and vain genealogies, which serve rather to controversies, as the apostle said, than to God's work of building up in the faith. By their craftily constructed rhetoric they lead astray the minds of

the inexperienced, and take them captive, corrupting the oracles of the Lord, and being evil expounders of what was well spoken.[14]

In contrast to the deceptive strategies of the heretics, the orthodox church is known by its unanimity:

> Having received this preaching and this faith, as I have said, the Church, although scattered in the whole world, carefully preserves it, as if living in one house. She believes these things [everywhere] alike, as if she had but one heart and one soul, and she preaches them harmoniously, and teaches them, and hands them down, as if she had but one mouth. For the languages of the world are different, but the meaning of the [Christian] tradition is one and the same.[15]

Patriarchal discourse is hierarchic, dualistic discourse; everything can be accounted for in two categories of existence: the dominant category and then everything else. This discourse has no place for diversity or difference. In fact, difference itself becomes a problem in this context. To diverge from the "tradition"(A) is to cross over into "heresy" (Not-A). The Christian orthodox voice is one voice, speaking one word. "One Lord, one faith, one baptism . . ." "We believe in one God, the Father, the Almighty, . . ." Indeed, as Irenaeus suggests, it was precisely this univocality which was itself the strongest evidence of orthodoxy. Thus divergence itself is the strongest evidence of heterodoxy.

Women are particularly identified with heresy and heterodoxy, since they already exist on the chaotic side of the dichotomy and are weak and thus subject to the temptations of heretical thinking and behavior. Heretical groups are identifiable by the prominence of women in them; women are seen as a prime source of heresy, already in the biblical Christian writings. Second Timothy cautions against heretics who "make their way into households and captivate silly women, overwhelmed by their sins and swayed by all kinds of desires, who are always being instructed and can never arrive at a knowledge of the truth" (II Timothy 3:6). For the author of Second Timothy, it is women's stupidity and foolishness that leads them into heresy. The author of the Book of Revelation sees women not as weak but as diabolically powerful and dangerous:

> But I have this against you: you tolerate that woman Jezebel, who calls herself a prophet and is teaching and beguiling my servants

24

to practice fornication and to eat food sacrificed to idols. I gave her
time to repent, but she refuses to repent of her fornication. Beware,
I am throwing her on a bed, and those who commit adultery with
her I am throwing into great distress, unless they repent of her
doings; and I will strike her children dead. (Revelation 2:20-23a)

In the ideology of this text, a woman teaching and preaching and
praying in public is a whore and a heretic. Heresy is read as
fornication, unfaithfulness; the loose woman's punishment is her
rape and her children's (probably meaning her followers') murder. Later in the same text the archenemy of the church (probably
Rome) is personified as a whore, on whose forehead is written
the legend, "Babylon the great, mother of whores and of earth's
abominations." (Revelation 17:5b) Later Christian anti-heretical
writings take up this theme of women as archetypal heretics, and
the association of heresy with sexual promiscuity to accuse other
Christians. Thus female leadership or public identity of any kind
becomes by definition heretical and sexual. Women are typically
heterodox and speak heteroglossia.

It should be noted at this point that what is being described
here is a particular strategy of dealing with difference deriving
from a particular logical perspective. As Nancy Jay remarked,
"They [A/Not-A dichotomies] are social creations, not supported
by any natural order, and as such, continual work is required to
maintain them."[16] The identification of Christian orthodoxy with
univocality is purely theoretical; it does not describe the reality
of the church during those periods or any other, since the church
has always been diverse and pluriform, and orthodoxy and heresy have always been categories with considerable slippage in
reality.[17] What it does describe is the attempt to maintain (or
restore) a certain social order. That this effort is still being attempted is demonstrated by the publication of a recent book, a
collection of articles entitled *The Politics of Prayer: Feminist Language and the Worship of God*. The cover and the epigraph indicate
the perspective of the contributors and editor: the cover depicts
the building of the Tower of Babel, and the epigraph cites the
same biblical story. The editor describes the book as an attempt
to respond to "conflict over objective religious truth." The contributors are concerned about "the effect of the continuing (and
currently intensified) politicization of those translations [of Bible
and liturgy] which has relativized the truth."[18]

Here the dichotomy is not overtly between orthodoxy and heresy, but truth against politicization, i. e., falsehood. It is worth noting that the arena which the contributors focus on is not biblical study or academic theology, but worship and ritual; more precisely, prayer. It is feminists who are the primary source of dangerous (polluting?), untrue, nonobjective "politicization" of prayer. Indeed, the charge of politicization suggests pollution, that is, the violation of boundaries: [orthodox, or "true"] prayer is A; politics [i.e., feminist concerns and critiques] are Not-A. When feminist concerns are introduced into prayer, the "excluded middle" is violated; prayer is polluted.

Liturgically speaking, this striving for unity and for control of women can be seen in such defenses of "true" worship by means of the creation or defense of "official" fixed liturgical texts. The *Didache* already proposes a pattern and text for Christian prayer along with its "Two Ways" teaching. The rubrics accompanying the text reflect a recognition that the words of a prophet cannot be controlled, but in providing the text and instructions, it also recognizes the untenability of the free prophet in a church that is beginning to define itself over and against others and to see freedom as a problem.[19] The rubrics following the eucharistic texts in the third-century document called the *Apostolic Tradition* make it clear that one purpose of providing the text is to control the content of this public prayer. Moreover, these early attempts at unification of the church's public prayer coincide with repression of women's leadership and identification of women with heresy.

But the striving for a unified voice is never completely successful (only death is truly unified in absolute silence). There are cracks and fissures in patriarchal discourse, through which other forms and models of discourse may be glimpsed or heard. This tendency toward a unified voice, however, means that these alternative models and voices must be relegated to the margins or trivialized, if they cannot be silenced or suppressed. The use of unitary language and discourse then easily becomes a strategy as well as a philosophical view. The unitary voice becomes a defense against critics and attackers, confirmation of group identity, a means of setting and defending boundaries.

This strategy can be observed in action any time the church perceives itself to be attacked or challenged. Of course, the question of what constitutes an attack or a challenge arises. As Nancy

Jay observes, the principle of A/Not-A dichotomy "is necessarily distorting when it is applied directly to the empirical world, for there are no negatives there. Everything that exists (including women), exists positively."[20] But for an institution defending itself against the threat of heterodoxy, or heteroglossia, these are threats precisely because they break the false unity of A. The danger of this dichotomous hierarchical thinking, then, is that it warps the church's view of itself and of those it defines as outside of itself. It leads the church to draw the circle smaller and smaller, to guard its identity jealously, to regard questions and diverse voices as attacks and challenges and as by definition belonging "outside the circle." Unitary thinking and praying requires conformity. That which does not conform must be dangerous, polluting, leading toward chaos, evil, "politicizing."

The church, then, as a patriarchal institution, desires to employ a prayer discourse which is unitary, both theologically and expressively. What I mean by this is that the conventions of traditional public prayer, understood as address by a community to God, value authorized speaking, controlled prayer, one model of God, and one model of address to that God, varieties of verbal expression and theoretical interpretations notwithstanding. Again, note that the church can only *desire* this univocality. The reality of the diversity of participants, the passage of time, the inevitable process of change in language, culture, and social context means that the maintenance of univocality is a constant effort.[21]

An objection to this critique of univocal prayer as patriarchal and oppressive might be raised by arguing that the striving for univocality is in fact a striving for universality, as a desire that, in the prayer of Christ, "all may be one, as I and the Father are one" (John 17:23). Solving disagreement and achieving unity and agreement is a good and desirable thing. Too much emphasis on difference and diversity can only splinter people into myriad small like-minded groups, with only their own concerns at heart. However, as Catharine MacKinnon notes, what often presents itself as universal is universal only at the cost of suppression of difference, not resolution:

> Many readers say that if a discourse is not generalized, universal, and agreed-upon, it is exclusionary. The problem, however, is that

27

the generalized, universal, agreed-upon never did solve the disagreement, resolve the differences, cohere the specifics, and generalize the particularities. Rather, it assimilated them to a false universal that imposed agreement, submerged specificity, and silenced particularity. The anxiety about engaged theory is particularly marked among those whose particularities formed the prior universal. What they face from this critique is not losing a dialogue but beginning one, a more equal and larger and inclusionary one. They do face losing the advance exclusivity of their point of view's claim to truth—that is, their power.[22]

Universalizing discourse, presenting a partial perspective as if it were the universal perspective, is false and misleading. To the extent that the striving for univocality is a striving for universality, it fails in its attempt. Univocal prayer tradition suppresses the dissenting voice, the view from the margin, the different speech, heteroglossia, and the movement toward diversity and richness.

Public Prayer, Private Women

A move toward feminist public prayer is made more difficult by the public/private dichotomy. A corollary to the male/female dichotomy which sees men as public is the identification of women with the private sphere, as if the two were discontinuous, and the private world were simply an absence of the public. The limitation of women to the private sphere (it is never a world) is typical of patriarchal culture more generally. Specifically, it has meant the association of women in the same class as other nonpublic persons: children and slaves. While the limited nature of this sphere seems to be in conflict with the idea that women are Not-A, and therefore are unlimited and chaotic, it is in fact this chaotic character of women (and children, and other "lesser" humans) which demands restrictions, "for her own good." The association of women with the private sphere delegitimizes any public action by women. Women who act in public are, it is said, acting on their Not-A nature, that is, weak, dangerous, uncontrolled, defiling. A public woman is a prostitute, a defiled and defiling creature, according to this patriarchal dichotomy.

But public prayer is just that: public. Authoritative Christian texts forbid women to pray in public, or insist on symbols of subordination (such as head coverings) to legitimate such dangerous, liminal behavior. How, then, can women claim the power to pray in public, to create forms and symbols to carry the meaning of the desires of our hearts to God before the community? Any words, any symbols that women create will be private by patriarchal definition. How can these "private" prayers be moved into the public sphere? Or is it better to ask, perhaps, how the wall that divides public and private can be dismantled?

The notion of the "private" deserves further examination. Feminist analysis has insisted on understanding the personal as political. Personal, private life has political meaning for women, whose most serious harm originates in the so-called private sphere because this is where rape, battery, incest, and abuse take place. As Catharine MacKinnon notes, for women the private sphere is "the distinctive sphere of intimate violation and abuse, neither free nor particularly personal."[23] In other words, the so-called right to privacy has more often functioned to make women's well-being more difficult to assure, not less. To cite MacKinnon again: "When women are segregated in private, separated from one another one at a time, a right to *that* privacy isolates women from each other and from public recourse. This right to privacy is a right of men 'to be let alone' to oppress women one at a time."[24]

This separation and privatization has religious and spiritual consequences for women. Although in the larger society religious practice is often itself seen as part of the private sphere, this is a misconception based on the nineteenth-century feminization of religion. Clearly, going to church is a public event. Praying in church is a public event. However, the full participation of women and children (and in white-dominated churches, of people of color) is forbidden or sharply limited. Anxiety about propriety and good order tends to fuel these limitations, betraying the assumption that women, children, and people of color of both genders and all ages are likely to behave improperly or shamefully (Not-A). Both conservative and fundamentalist churches invoke the public/private dichotomy used in Christian scriptural texts:

(As in all the churches of the saints, women should be silent in the churches. For they are not permitted to speak, but should be subordinate, as the law says. If there is anything they desire to know, *let them ask their husbands at home*. For it is shameful for a woman to speak in church.) (I Corinthians 14:33*b*-35; emphasis added; parenthesis in NRSV)

The A/Not-A dichotomy of the public/private split is clear in this text; women are to limit their speaking to the private sphere, in order to maintain their subordination in public. This text also makes the covert subordination and domination of the public/private split overt. The maintenance of the public (A) and private (not-A) realms is a means of maintaining male dominance and female (and non-free male) subordination.

For a woman to transgress this barrier between public and private is to disrupt the dichotomy and to pollute the public realm. Janice Raymond notes, "For men, any free and independent woman signals a 'loose woman.' The freedom of women is equated with whoredom."[25] A woman speaking in public, a woman speaking freely, a woman knowing her mind and speaking it freely to God in public, is, in patriarchal society and masculinist religion, a loose woman. She has broken loose from religious and cultural limitations. She crosses boundaries of public and private and disrupts the discourse of the fathers. She will be called a whore; in patriarchal religious context, a whore is a heretic, a heretic is a whore.

Feminist Creation of Multiple Meanings

Many women who are grounded in the Christian tradition have spent much of their religious lives in radical acts of translation of the tradition. One might well ask, At what cost?

Elisabeth Castelli, "Les Belles Infidèles/Fidelity or Feminism?"[26]

Women engage in constant translation during Christian prayer, putting ourselves in where we never were, or seeing the shades of women before us whose words were forgotten, suppressed, denied. We need language for prayer; as Adrienne Rich says, "This is the oppressor's language yet I need it to talk to you."[27]

The alternative to univocality is *heteroglossia*: other languages, different tongues. In order to be heard, the new voices must do two things simultaneously: create a new language and seek legitimation for the new language alongside the old, unitary language. This will be seen as a threat to unitary thinking, and it is. For the new voice to be granted legitimacy, the principle of unitary voice must be abandoned or so severely redefined that it is scarcely recognizable. Institutions spend a lot of time monitoring these new voices, and will always want to redefine or reshape the new voice to be compatible with the old, in order to preserve the unitary principle.

The process of creating multiple meanings in what is essentially a unitary context requires strategy. What I call "praying between the lines" is a strategy of survival and resistance. I mean by this phrase both something quite strategic and also something more metaphorical. As a strategy it is commonly employed by many women and some men for protecting themselves from spiritual and psychic (and sometimes professional) damage and for surviving in the church. As a metaphor, it refers to the struggle for inclusion of certain voices, or certain relationships, or certain perspectives within the conversation with God that is the purpose of public prayer. It is another form of "translation" in which women and disempowered men are continually engaged. It is usually internal (although in a unison prayer or perhaps a sung prayer, an alternative expression might be voiced). It is a strategy of resistance, and therefore engages us in discussions about power, both human and divine. It is one manifestation of what researchers Miriam Therese Winter, Adair Lummis, and Alison Stokes call "defecting in place."[28] One of their informants observed,

> The exclusive language of the liturgy, which I do love, always presents a challenge. Perhaps Episcopalians will one day begin to worship inclusively. Until then, I'll translate the liturgy for myself, not unlike I once did when worshipping in Chinese while living in Taiwan. How sad that many women in worship feel like strangers in a strange land.[29]

This kind of translation challenges, albeit not always openly, the institutional churches' preference for unitary, or univocal, prayer, by praying not from the position of "A", within controlled limits, but from the position of "Not-A", the limitless, the free space of rich and varied heteroglossia. From this position, the "A" position seems like a strange land.

I offer two contemporary examples of this praying between the lines. An Anglican priest in Canada tells me that the most significant words in the Eucharistic prayer for her are when she says the words, "this is my body," "this is my blood." However, they are significant to her not for the expected traditional pious or orthodox doctrinal reasons. She accepts no patriarchal reading of the text. Rather, as she explained to me, when speaking those words as priest in the midst of a congregation, in the context of the central liturgical act of her faith, she was able to hear and announce before her community an affirmation of her woman's body and her woman's blood.

It is my experience that this sort of counter-reading is very common among women and among other marginalized worshipers in our assemblies. We grow accustomed, as Elizabeth Castelli notes, to translating as we go, reading ourselves into the text from which we have been excised, by reading behind the texts, reading the silences and the spaces, the absences and the omissions. We learn to hear words not spoken aloud, see signs unread by others. And we learn to keep our readings to ourselves. The patriarchal desire for a unified reading is not patient of other readings or other languages.

In spite of this risk of exposure to the suppressive tactics of patriarchal power, some alternate readings are sometimes made explicit to the entire assembly. One such event was a mainline Protestant seminary chapel service observing rape awareness week on campus. In the context of a service drawing attention to violence against women, Psalm 140 was read in its noninclusive, literal form:

> Deliver me, O Lord, from evil men; preserve me from violent men,
> who plan evil things in their hearts. (Psalm 140: 1, 2a)

The context itself, by focusing on taboo matters having to do with women's bodies, was already an alternative context. Within that context, the feminist counter-reading of the psalm was made public, and it made public sense. It exposed the limitations of the generic male speech by demonstrating its specificity. It also invested traditional texts with new meaning, challenging unitary assumptions about meaning and interpretation. In its disruptive results, this strategy resembles bell hooks' use of black vernacular speech in academic settings:

> When I need to say words that do more than simply mirror or address the dominant reality, I speak black vernacular. There, in that location, we make English do what we want it to do. We take

the oppressor's language and turn it against itself. We make our words a counter-hegemonic speech, liberating ourselves in language.[30]

Women who read themselves into the prayers of the church, whether privately or publicly, are creating a "counter-hegemonic speech," freeing themselves through language, making the language of prayer "do what we want it to do," in the specific instance just cited, speaking the truth about men's violence against women.

This creation of counter-speech, when articulated publicly, may not be immediately understood and accepted by those whose primary speech is the dominant speech. Writing about the valuing of black vernacular, bell hooks observes,

> Now that the audience for feminist writing and speaking has become more diverse, it is evident that we must change conventional ways of thinking about language, creating spaces where diverse voices can speak in words other than English or in broken, vernacular speech. This means that at a lecture or even in a written work there will be fragments of speech that will not be accessible to every individual.[31]

The public articulation of "praying between the lines" suggests that the same may at times be true of Christian prayer. Although the univocal prayer claims to speak for all, the existence of different "translations" of one univocal prayer makes it clear that it does not. Current "unison" or "corporate" prayer is in fact not "accessible to every individual"; it is not in fact one voice, one body, but many voices, many bodies, many of whom are praying between the lines.

The difficulty of overt "praying between the lines" for many Christian women is not lack of understanding but threat of charges of heresy. Public prayer is not simply public speech (although women engaging in public speech is problematic enough), but it is highly charged speech, speech with God, and claiming to represent a community of people. At a national conference celebrating the World Council of Churches' Decade in Solidarity with Women, women's prayers moved out from their usual place "between the lines" of official church prayers and into public view. In particular, prayers addressed to Sophia/God, celebrating the holiness of women's bodies aroused the outrage of conservative Christian activists who charged the organizers and participants with heresy and attacked them personally and professionally. The assertion that the functions of women's bodies are holy, and the celebration of that holiness in symbols of milk and honey, challenged simultaneously the hegemony of Christian praying and the historic Christian hatred and fear of women's bodies. Making space for this kind of speech, which honors women and voices what has been denied, is costly and dangerous, as the participants and planners at the Re-Imagining Conference discovered. The creation of multiple meanings is deeply threatening to patriarchal univocality. Nancy Jay's observation is pertinent here:

> One cannot but be struck by the enormous amount of social effort expended, of sustained, cooperative work performed, and of oppression and violence done in the creation and maintenance of such social dichotomies.[32]

The reaction against the conference also demonstrates the need for women-church gatherings, and has created an ongoing "Re-Imagining Community," a network of support for women creating spaces for themselves and their prayer.

Less dramatically, most women simply find themselves isolated. This Episcopal laywoman describes reaction to her modest attempts to use inclusive language in Scripture readings:

> It feels as though feminist spirituality, in a place like this, is an underground thing—like being a secret dissident or something. Maybe if I lived somewhere where heterogeneity was accepted (or was the norm!), it would be easier to "come out" as a religious feminist. As it is, it's pretty lonely most of the time.[33]

She identifies clearly the need for heterogeneity. In a context hostile to heterogeneity, she also recognizes the survival need for secrecy, for private "praying between the lines."

Multiple Meanings and Internal Dissent

The presence of multiple meanings in the liturgical text is recognized by those erased or marginalized by the text, but feared by those for whom the text must be bound to a single meaning. Nancy Jay remarks,

Those whose understanding of society [and church] is ruled by such an ideology find it very hard to conceive of the possibility of alternative forms of social [or religious] order (third possibilities). Within such thinking, the only alternative to the one order is disorder.[34]

The only alternative to the one true meaning of the text, to the one true form of prayer, to orthodoxy (literally, "correct praise"), is falsehood, heresy, heterodoxy (literally, "other praise").

Alternative readings and intentional omissions suggest critique, even when that critique remains unarticulated aloud. Praying between the lines is ultimately disruptive, whether that disruption makes itself known in public ways or is felt only in the heart of the woman who finds herself engaged in the process.

Much traditional ritual analysis has assumed that a critical attitude is inimical to the doing of ritual in general and to public praying in particular. Ritual is understood to be a bodily experience and therefore separate from cognitive activities such as analysis, critical thinking, and the like. The body, this interpretation argues, is precognitive and therefore precritical. Ritual theorist Ronald Grimes has pointed out the problem with this assumption, namely, that the body is not mindless; the mind is part of the body. Instead, the "ritualizing body" is capable of "creative, cognitive, critical functions."[35] Feminists would add that women may be particularly aware of the critical abilities of the body, given not only our cultural and religious identification with bodiliness, but also our (culturally and religiously imposed) attention to the cycles and functions of our bodies as sources of danger and pollution, as well as our own sense (however fragile) of our bodies as sources of pleasure and pride. The natural cycles and responses of our bodies as women tell us not only that our bodies are cognitive, but also that the knowledge of our bodies is suppressed knowledge. An element, perhaps the central element in that body knowledge, is the knowledge that women are socially, legally, and religiously unequal to men on the basis of sex. In male-dominated society, our bodies are always threatened with intrusion and violence, even though that intrusion and violence is regarded culturally and religiously as unremarkable. As MacKinnon notes, "As sexual inequality is gendered as man and woman, gender inequality is sexualized as dominance and subordination."[36] The existence of pornography, and the prevalence of rape and battery of women, construct the body knowledge of women. Our bodies are not ours to define, to claim, to protect, or to enjoy.

Instead, our bodies know fear and threat of harm and invasion. Our bodies are seen as polluting, but in fact what we know is that our bodies are used, abused, and polluted. Our bodies are seen as dangerous, but we know that it is others who are a danger to our bodies. This body knowledge criticizes the patriarchal interpretation of our bodies: not dangerous, but endangered.

Grimes notes that embedded criticism is not alien to ritual. "Criticism itself can take the form of an action, a gesture. It need not take the form of an intellectual operation separate from ritual performance."[37] The woman who remains silent during the singing of a hymn with a sexist text engages in ritual criticism; the woman who changes the words of a unison prayer as she reads engages in ritual criticism; the woman who refuses communion to protest her tradition's denial of women's access to ordination engages in ritual criticism. These forms of embedded criticism become the seedbed of the creation of feminist rituals, which are thus simultaneously critiques of existing traditional forms of religious ritual and new creations designed to respond positively to the critique.

Joan Radner and Susan S. Lanser, in a study of feminist coded messages in folklore, have developed a typology of coding strategies that sheds light on the liturgical strategies I am drawing attention to here.[38]

Appropriation (also called "symbolic inversion" or "mimicry") adapts patriarchal designations in exaggerated and ironic form. This is a strategy similar to that proposed by biblical scholar Jane Schaberg in translating misogynist New Testament texts:

> In contrast to inclusive translation, feminist translation as I see it would highlight the exclusion (at least the deliberate kind) and the androcentrism of the biblical text, would mimic and mock the loud male voice and tone, would turn up the volume on its evasions and lies and guilt, put dots and slashes to mark the gaps and omissions.[39]

Liturgically, this strategy might be seen in some women's appropriation and reinterpretation of traditional "Women's Days" in church, in which all liturgical leadership roles, normally held by men, are taken by women. Although in its uncoded (or unreflected) form these occasions are tokenism in one of its purest forms, they sometimes also become, under the direction of women dissatisfied with such minimalization, strongly affirmative of women, temporarily displacing the patriarchal marginalization of women.

Juxtaposition involves the ironic placement of subversive messages in the context of patriarchal contexts. Liturgically, this might be seen in the use of female language for God in an otherwise traditional service, or the reading of biblical texts which demand subservience of women together with texts which emphasize freedom and equality. The most common example of juxtaposition in churches, however, also demonstrates the risks and ambiguity of this strategy: the presence of clergywomen as liturgical leaders. On the one hand, their presence tacitly challenges the centuries-long tradition that has marginalized women as religious leaders. On the other hand, their presence may also be read as affirmation by women of the very historical structures and practices that have kept women out of religious leadership and continue to make women's exercise of religious leadership difficult.

Distraction is a strategy illustrated by the African American slave practice of banging on pots to cover the sounds of the singing of hymns with subversive texts, such as "Oh Freedom."[40] It refers to the use of any sort of distraction—aural, textual, musical, verbal—which draws attention away from the subversive power of the message. A woman preaching, in defiance of tradition and teaching, may choose to dress very traditionally in order to distract the congregation from the subversive meaning of her presence or her message.

Indirection, according to Radner and Lanser, is the most common of all. They identify three forms: metaphorical indirection, impersonation, and hedging. All of these strategies involve distancing one's self from the subversive truth being told, taking protective coloration, so to speak, by use of metaphor, the identity of another (fictional?) character, or equivocation. Hymns which use male "generic" language offer numerous opportunities for metaphorical indirection. A form of indirection commonly used by religious women is to disavow responsibility for transgressions of religious gender codes by claiming divine inspiration.

Trivialization involves the use of "a form, mode or genre that the dominant culture considers unimportant, innocuous, or irrelevant."[41] Trivialization as a strategy frequently involves the use of humor, which serves to defuse and to some extent distract from the subversive character of the message. In a study by folklorist Elaine Lawless on women in the pulpit, a clergywoman describing a clergywomen's newsletter, remarks,

> We wanted to call our newsletter "Naked in the Pulpit" because that's the way we were feeling much of the time, so since we couldn't, we called it "Notions 'n Pins"—the NIP still stands for "naked in the pulpit," but nobody knows that.[42]

Claiming or demonstrating incompetence in traditional female tasks (such as cooking, sewing, making coffee) functions practically to save women from being expected to perform such tasks. It also functions symbolically to challenge the patriarchal assignment of gender-based roles. Claims of incompetence can also serve as distraction or camouflage for nontraditional activities a woman may already be doing. Such claims of incompetence are commonplace in women's literature. Elaine Lawless has drawn attention to similar claims employed by Pentecostal women preachers, who must disguise their competent exercise of religious power as a response to an irresistible call from God, rather than any merit or skill of their own, and insist on their personal incompetence.[43]

The Limitations of Private Meanings

> For all the ingenious uses women, or any dominated peoples, may make of coding, then, the need for coding must always signify a freedom that is incomplete.
>
> Joan Radner and Susan Lanser, *Strategies of Coding*

Praying between the lines is a strategy which disrupts patriarchal unitary prayer language; but because it is a strategy which is often coded, and thus camouflaged within patriarchal discourse, its power to disrupt is limited. Joanna Dewey remarks, regarding this and all sorts of "translations" women are regularly engaged in,

> This is a matter of survival, and not in itself threatening to the powers that be. But when we band together and propose/attempt/

do feminist translation of the tradition, rendering the tradition available to women already translated, already in a form that does not require each individual to do her own translating, but rather establishes her as someone having voice, then indeed translation becomes an act of political subversion.[44]

Moving from coded strategies to disruptive and reconstructive strategies is necessary in order to make room for freedom.

Strategies such as "praying between the lines," which retain the camouflage of outer convention, raise the question of what changes in conventions of prayer need to take place to render such camouflage unnecessary. What strategies are most likely to bring about such changes in the church's public prayer? What must happen in order for women to be free to address God truthfully in public prayer?

BESTOWING OURSELVES TO SILENCE
The Prayer of Refusal

If 'no' can be taken as 'yes,' how free can 'yes' be?

Catharine MacKinnon, *Toward a Feminist Theory of the State*

Development of alternative, subversive readings of univocal prayers is a strategy of survival and resistance. It is a covert way of offering critique, of saying *no* to certain prayers, to certain assumptions, to certain postures and attitudes of prayer. But the generating of feminist liturgical prayer requires moving from coded strategies to overt strategies that disrupt the harmful dichotomous conventional prayer discourse and create the space necessary for the creation of reconstructive strategies of prayer. This requires saying *no to* prayer and *no in* prayer.

Saying *no to* univocal prayer disrupts the contradictory dichotomy of A/Not-A. It also claims the power of the fast: a recognition that there is power in refusal and negation. Saying *no in* prayer resists not only the conventions of traditional prayer, but also resists traditional assumptions about God's omnipotence and beneficence, and resists God. But the Christian prayer tradition offers few resources for saying no in prayer, and none for saying no to prayer. Moreover, the social and religious expectations placed on women deny us the vocabulary for saying no. How do we discover and ritualize in prayer our *no*?

The Necessity of Saying No

Univocal prayer creates a coercive space in which consent is assumed and *yes* is the only possible response. Christian liturgy,

41

and especially Christian prayer, presumes consent. That is to say, our practices of prayer and ritual presume the agreement of the participants, and assume that the participants are capable of consent. Prayers of confession and declarations of faith in particular make this presumption:

> Almighty and most merciful God,
> we confess that we have sinned against you
> by thought, word, and deed. . . .
>
> I believe in one God, the Father Almighty. . . .

Unitary prayer presents the participants with texts which do not need to ask ("Do you believe?" "Have you sinned?") because they begin from the presumption of consent: "Say what you believe." "Confess your sins."

But the notion of consent is problematic for women. Legal theorist Catharine MacKinnon considers the idea of consent in connection with rape law and abortion law. She notes:

> The law of rape presents consent as free exercise of sexual choice under conditions of equality of power without exposing the underlying structure of constraint and disparity. Fundamentally, desirability to men is supposed to be women's form of power because she can both arouse it and deny its fulfillment. . . . This rationalizes force. Consent in this model becomes more a metaphysical quality of a woman's being than a choice she makes and communicates. Exercise of women's so-called power presupposes more fundamental social powerlessness.[1]

African American feminists have also questioned the idea of universal consent, and its underlying presumption of free exercise of free will, from the perspective of women living under systems of racial slavery and oppression.[2] Those whose choices and behaviors are constrained by systems of oppression—by white supremacy and male domination—cannot be said to exercise free choice, and thus their possibility of granting consent is compromised. At the same time, because they cannot be said to have any consent to offer, since consent does not have be established, implicit consent becomes part of what is regarded as their nature: "a metaphysical quality of a woman's being." Survival under conditions of oppression demands skills of acquiescence, of what Katie Cannon calls "invisible dignity, quiet grace, and unshouted courage."[3] As MacKinnon notes, women's consent,

42

our *yes*, is always presumed, even when we in fact say *no*. But saying no and being heard is essential to our survival, to our lives as beings in the world. To harm and violence and exploitation and repression we must say no. To say no for others is expected of us, especially of women, but we must say it for ourselves. As Marge Piercy says, in "Unlearning not to speak":

> She must learn again to speak
> starting with *I*
> starting with *We*
> starting as an infant does
> with her own true hunger
> and pleasure
> and rage.[4]

In the church especially, women's "no" has been limited, suppressed, and denied. Louise Erdrich speaks of this suppression of women's *no* as "veiling," and reimagines her own confirmation as a ritual of saying no, of rejecting the veiling, the suppression, the silencing:

> . . . I have rehearsed over and over in air and in the mirror the act of tipping my head back, eyes shut and tongue out, receiving Christ.
> To keep my mouth shut. To turn away my face. To walk back down the aisle. To slap the bishop back when he slapped me during confirmation. To hold the word *no* in my mouth like a gold coin, something valuable, something possible. To teach the *no* to our daughters. To value their *no* more than their compliant *yes*. To celebrate *no*. To hold the word *no* in your fist and refuse to give it up. To support the boy who says *no* to violence, the girl who will not be violated, the woman who says *no, no, no. I will not*. To love the *no*, to cherish the *no*, which is so often our first word. *No*—the means to transformation.[5]

Erdrich admits that "it takes about a decade of wild blue dancing" to shed one veil, to learn to love and cherish our *no*. Even longer, one might suspect, if one is deeply invested in traditional Christian piety in which Jesus does not say no to his own suffering and death, in which the women saints and martyrs, heroines of the faith, are remembered for their compliance in the face of suffering and not their resistance.

After being raised in a free-church, nonliturgical tradition, I discovered the Episcopal church as an adult and fell under the enchantment of its stately ritual. As it happened, the church I chose to join for its elaborate ritual was also one of the most conservative in town; famous, in fact, for its conservatism. This in a diocese known for its conservatism, in a denomination identified with wealth and prestige for hundreds of years. Be that as it may, the ritual of this church moved me deeply, answered a hunger I did not even know I had. I requested confirmation. But as the time of confirmation by the bishop drew near, the priest teaching our Inquirer's Class mentioned in passing at the conclusion of a session that the women and girls being confirmed would wear a lace head covering for the occasion. I don't know why this shocked me so, since I had noticed that many (not all) of the women who attended the church wore little lace doilies on their heads. I suppose that to the extent I thought about it at all, I thought it represented a fashion choice rather than a religious statement.

Surprised somewhat at my own temerity, I approached the priest after class, and asked the reason for the requirement. He murmured something about St. Paul and First Corinthians. Well, I knew all about that; I was a seminary student at the time; I had taken courses in New Testament, even in the writings of Paul. I knew higher criticism, and I explained to the priest why this was a dubious interpretation of Paul at best. But what I knew at a level I could scarcely articulate to myself, let alone this priest, was that this requirement was insulting to me. I could not, would not, wear anything even remotely resembling a veil. *No*, I said. *No*. The priest was somewhat taken aback, but did not argue. So I went to be presented to the bishop, among the little girls with their lace doilies, bareheaded. Not yet loving and cherishing my *no*, but doing it nevertheless, transforming my relationship with the church forever.

The triviality of my modest struggle to say no contrasts with the life-and-death struggles of women with less privilege. Sister Mary John Mananzan, OSB, records accounts of some Filipino women's struggles to remove the "veils" and begin to cherish their no, in contexts not only of gender oppression, but also of racism, colonialism, and other forms of violence.[6] In these stories, compliance is spiritualized, as is male dominance and female submission, as is white Western domination and oppression.

Lourdes San Agustin[7] describes the spiritualization of patriarchal compliance:

> I grew up in a family that was patriarchal—my father was the dominant figure, my mother, as well as we, the children, were obedient, submissive, and passive. . . . At times, my mother would tell me do not do that, do not do this because Papa Jesus will get angry. So, at an early age, my notion of God was male, just like my father, who also should be pleased and obeyed.

The demands of compliance and obedience, the threat of anger, are demands that nurture patriarchal prayer and justify the relationships of the patriarchal household.

Ka Odeng, reporting in Pampango, from which her account was translated into English, describes her progress in learning to say *no* not only to her oppression as a woman but also to her oppression as a poor woman, a peasant woman, living under violent military oppression:

> I am a peasant woman. I was born to a poor family, the seventh among thirteen children. We were a religious family. Every Sunday my mother would take us, all thirteen children, to church to pray that God may give us his grace. In spite of our faithfulness, we continued to be poor and to suffer. In my mind, the question echoed and re-echoed: why are we still poor? My grandparents kept telling my parents, especially my mother, that we were poor because we still did not pray enough. The contradiction is that we have been praying, we have not done anything evil or wrong, yet nothing has changed. We are as impoverished as ever. . . .

Ka Odeng, rejecting the spiritualization of her poverty, joined a study group discussing land reform. Over her family's objections and fears, she began to understand the political and social forces keeping her family poor. She began to lead groups herself, and to organize other women.

> At 17 I got married, I have 5 children. My husband and I had been organizers in our village. . . .
>
> My husband was killed by the military. . . . His death came as a shock to me. The military treated him like a pig. They told him he was too smart so they hacked his head. . . . His arm was cut off because the military said he had been trying to teach the village folk. His legs were broken and then cut off because they said he

had been going around to the whole province, teaching his fellow peasants to become strong before their oppressors.

He pleaded for his life and said, "Don't kill me, think of my family." In spite of that, they killed him.

Now, in spite of what the military had done, I have committed myself to the cause of our people. . . .

As a woman, I pursue my task of organizing other peasant women, inspiring them to play significant roles in society and to gain dignity and identity. . . . I have learned in my life that it is not enough to pray. One has to do something if only to become free.

An Ifugao woman, called "Sister Jannie," describes her struggle to recognize the power of her native religious tradition in spite of the suppression and demonization of that religious identity by representatives of Christianity:

I belong to one of the tribes of the Cordillera—the Ifugaos. We are usually portrayed in the lowlands as pagans, headhunters, ignorant, uncivilized, with tails, etc. . . .

The baptismal certificate I acquired before entering the convent testifies that I was baptized a few days after I was born. I was given a saintly European name. . . . We were made to understand that Christian names were more acceptable, superior, and more pleasing to the ear. . . . I had to pray the rosary doubly hard and I offered a lot of sacrifices for the repose of the souls of my ancestors who died without baptism, without Christian names. . . .

She also recalls vividly, and reproduces for the book, a picture from Parish School which depicts "Heaven: for good, obedient children," "Limbo: for pagans," "Hell: for bad children." A teacher holds a drawing of a huge eye and says, "Children there are 3 persons in one God. God sees everything and likes obedient children." She comments:

Such lessons were very successful in mystifying and domesticating the animist within us. This spirit was eventually alienated from my tribal nature. I became passive and sometimes confused. Soon I lost my capacity to rely on collective efforts to face the daily problems that confronted us as children. I became an individualist and developed a moralistic attitude. . . . I realize now that I had a "split spirituality": The "Christian" in me claimed to be superior, right and dogmatic. But deep down in my gut, the tribal spirit was telling me that there was something wrong, something alien. Within me, that spirit was rebelling.

The spiritualization of dominance and submission as male and female roles, the uses of a spirituality of submission and compliance for social, religious, and political repression and violence, and the passivity inculturated by certain types of Christian piety all suppress the *no* of women and of all oppressed people. All three of these accounts question prayer: its efficacy, its direction, its consequences. "It is not enough to pray; one must do something if only to be free," concludes Ka Odeng. Sister Jannie experiences the questioning as her animist spirit "in her gut," a resistance to individualism and moral rigidity as well as a resistance to denial of her identity. Prayer in the experiences of these women is not transformative because it does not leave room for the transformative *no*. The use of strategies of encoding, even though they would perhaps have reduced the risk each of these women faced, was rejected. Praying between the lines became unthinkable, undoable.

Prayer and Betrayal

A few years ago a woman student, a survivor of battering by her father and her older brother, told me matter-of-factly that she cannot close her eyes to pray in church, because she does not feel safe with her eyes closed.

Women who are survivors of violence, and women and men who work to end the violence, find themselves in a crisis of prayer. They frequently feel like illegitimate worshipers, since they are unable to have the loving, forgiving feelings expected of them, and they find it hard or impossible to affirm the faithfulness and goodness of God. Instead, they often feel anger at God and the church, and a deep sense of betrayal.

The anger and betrayal they feel is justified in the face of a church which is more often than not silent in the face of violence against women, a church which by its silence supports the violent man and fails his victims. In the face of this double betrayal (by one who has promised love, and by the church that has promised salvation) there are times when the patriarchal prayer discourse does not admit of subversive counter-readings. A prayer of confession confesses sin as disobedience and rebellion:

> We have failed to be an obedient church,
> we have not done your will . . .

47

> we have rebelled against your love . . .
> Forgive us, we pray.
> Free us for joyful obedience. . . .[8]

No subversive reading of "joyful obedience" is possible for a woman who lives in fear that her husband will kill her.[9] Most traditional postures of prayer are postures of submission: kneeling, prostrations, head bowed, eyes closed. They literally place the person in a physically vulnerable position. No subversive reading of this posture is possible to a woman who is regularly raped and beaten by her husband.

Patriarchal prayer discourse emphasizes the weakness, sinfulness, and ignorance of the one praying, and emphasizes the superior power, goodness, or wisdom of the one to whom we pray. No subversive reading of such discourse is possible for a woman who is constantly belittled, derided, and humiliated in public and private by her husband, her employer, or her colleagues. No alternative reading of this discourse is possible for women who are confronted daily with media images of women humiliated, exploited, or abused.

In other words, eventually one comes to times and circumstances in which a subversive counter-reading of a patriarchal prayer is not possible. The patriarchal reading of violence against women assigns it to certain times and circumstances. Violence against women, says the patriarchal male voice, is occasional, an aberration, an exception; on the whole, patriarchal gender arrangements are benign, good for most women. The feminist reading of male violence is the reverse. Male violence against women, as against other oppressed groups, is not exceptional, it is normal business-as-usual. It is paradigmatic of the meaning of life in patriarchal culture, and all women live with the threat of such violence always. This knowledge stops the prayer in the throat. The prayer of confession, the prayer of thanksgiving, the prayer of petition, have no meaning in the face of this knowledge. This knowledge, it must be emphasized, is also part and parcel of the knowledge of racism by the person of color, the knowledge of homophobia by the lesbian or gay person.

Is it surprising then that we bestow ourselves to silence, in the words of poet Adrienne Rich? When we "bestow ourselves to silence, or a severer listening" we hear in ourselves the very word that patriarchal power does not permit to us: the word is *no*. As

Catharine MacKinnon observes, if woman's *no* always can mean *yes*, what does her yes mean, or does it have any meaning at all? Until we can say *no* in truth, and let the no be received as *no*, we cannot say *yes*, for our yes is without content. We must choose the prayer of refusal.

Feminist liturgy groups rarely include anything resembling traditional prayer as public, oral address to God. This refusal to pray in conventional discourse arises out of this knowledge of suffering and struggle of women. It reflects, in varying degrees, anger and alienation toward traditional representations of God and toward churches and their representatives. It reflects doubt in the existence or beneficence of a God "out there." It reflects profound dissatisfaction with the traditional forms and practices of prayer. It reflects rejection of traditional prayer's habit of putting words into the mouths of others. Feminist liturgy groups refuse to pray in order to rehearse the necessary no, the refusal.

But in order to say no we must claim the power to speak, as Rebecca Chopp has termed it.[10] And in saying no to patriarchal prayer discourse, we grope for words, and we find them in prayers of lament and in prayers of anger. And here sometimes we do find resources between the lines of patriarchal prayer, in some of the psalms, in the almost forgotten tradition of lament, in rituals of exorcism and excommunication. And here too we find prayer taking new forms, outside the structures of patriarchal prayer discourse.

Prayer and Women's Anger

And, above all other prohibitions, what has been forbidden to women is anger, together with the open admission of the desire for power and control over one's life (which inevitably means accepting some degree of power and control over other lives).

Carolyn Heilbrun, *Writing a Woman's Life*

As Carolyn Heilbrun suggests, the exercise of anger and control are problematic for women. Philosopher Marilyn Frye calls the connection between anger and control "domain":

Anger implies a claim to domain—a claim that one is a being whose purposes and activities require and create a web of objects, space, attitudes and interests that is worthy of respect, and that the topic of this anger is a matter rightly within that web.[11]

What is regarded as appropriately part of women's—or a woman's—domain determines the level of acceptance a woman's anger will receive, the extent to which it will be taken seriously, a reaction Frye calls "uptake":

> . . . in each of our lives, others' concepts of us are revealed by the limits of the intelligibility of our anger. Anger can be an instrument of cartography. By determining where, with whom, about what and in what circumstances one can get angry and get uptake, one can map others' concepts of who and what one is.[12]

What map emerges when we ask these questions of women in Christianity, women and prayer? Whose anger is recognized as legitimate, whose rejected? Where is anger allowed, where disallowed? The resulting map would show that anger of the inferior is not allowed at the superior. This means that women's anger at men is not allowed or recognized as legitimate; but it also means that anger at God or at the church is not allowed or legitimate. Seminary students react with horror when I suggest that even feeling (let alone expressing) anger at God might be legitimate and even healthy in some circumstances.

Legitimate anger is externalized: at men, at the way of the world, at the church, at God. Internalized, it becomes depression, illness, despair, self-destruction. Externalized anger, then, is a gift we give ourselves, although it is directed outward. In order to engender feminist liturgical prayer and externalize our legitimate anger, we must claim the churches, their liturgy and prayer, and our relationship with God as our proper domain. We must create a noncoercive space where the *no* of our anger can be articulated and can receive uptake, can be received as legitimate.

Feminist ethicist Beverly Wildung Harrison argues that anger is an essential element in moral loving action. For Harrison, anger has two functions: it signals a serious relational problem, and it provides the energy to undertake the necessary work of restoring the relationship:

> . . . anger is—and it always is—a sign of some resistance in ourselves to the moral quality of the social relations in which we are immersed. Extreme and intense anger signals a deep reaction to the

action upon us or toward others to whom we are related. To grasp this point—that anger signals something amiss in relationship—is a critical first step in understanding the power of anger in the work of love. Where anger rises, there the energy to act is present.[13]

This energy to act for change is precisely the energy denied to women in the denial of women's anger.

In its ritualized form, articulation of anger is known as cursing. A curse is the opposite of a blessing. Like blessing, cursing presupposes the power and efficacy of the spoken (or written) word.[14] Curses and blessings are, in the terms of J. L. Austin, "performative speech," words which cause something to happen.[15] If a blessing recognizes and names holiness, then a curse recognizes and names evil. However, when a curse arises out of justified anger, the energy it embodies can bring about well-being and, ultimately, blessing. Alice Walker recognizes the redemptive quality of curses in *The Color Purple*. Celie, the main character of the novel, is able, after years of abuse and misuse, to curse her husband Mr.———, naming the evil he has done to her. Her curse ultimately brings about his redemption.[16]

Related to curses are excommunication rites. These rites were developed by the church authorities to ban those who had offended against church teaching in some way. Intended to effect repentance and reconciliation, these rites were understood as medicinal. However, as used by authoritarian church officials, the rite of excommunication in particular became a political tool in the church's struggle for power against secular rulers during the middle ages. However, this ritual, originally intended to fortify univocality and monolithic identity and power, can be recontextualized to claim the diverse voice, the perspective from the margin. For example, *Equal Rites*, a collection of liturgies and rituals for lesbian and gay Christians, includes a "litany for divine intervention," based on the greater excommunication of the *Pontificale Romanum*. In an interesting example of the use of a ritual with oppressive meaning in the past as a means of emancipation in the present, this litany condemns "the earthly conduct, speech, and writings" of highly visible individuals who oppress gay and lesbian Christians. The interpretation accompanying this rite describes it as:

a ritual to express and channel justifiable anger and outrage, and to plead for divine intervention in combating falsehoods and heterosexist myths.[17]

In this ritual, the redemptive power of anger is claimed and ritualized not on behalf of the powerful but of the oppressed.

Among the earliest feminist rituals were exorcisms that adapted the traditional exorcism ritual of the church to feminist purposes, rejecting and banishing misogyny and violence against women, both in ancient texts and contemporary contexts.[18] Contemporary versions of the rite of exorcism are not readily accessible. The *Book of Common Prayer* includes a chapter, "Concerning Exorcism," in *The Book of Occasional Services*. The rite itself is not reproduced there, however, but only two paragraphs explaining that

> Very early in the life of the Church the development and exercise of such rites were reserved to the bishop, at whose discretion they might be delegated to selected presbyters and others deemed competent.[19]

These rites have been (and still are) used by patriarchal authority to reinforce and maintain patriarchal power.

Exorcisms, excommunications, and curses, all prayers that bring about what they speak, are traditional forms of liturgical expression of anger which claim domain for saying *no*. All of these rituals have been and continue to be in the control of patriarchal structures and leaders. Feminist appropriation of these patterns must recognize their misuse as well as their potential for creating a space for expression of women's anger in prayer.

Prayer and Women's Grief

> My heart is moved by all I cannot save: so much has been destroyed. . . .
>
> Adrienne Rich, "Natural Resources"[20]

Where is grief expressed in Christian prayer? Funeral liturgies emphasize hope and joy, do not linger on grief, mute the possibility of lament. Keening is not liturgically recognized in mainline Christian worship. Lament and rage often go together in the Psalms, but the psalm most frequently found in recommendations for funeral services is the twenty-third Psalm, which is not a lament, but a denial of grief: "I shall not want." But grief is desire

52

denied: I do want, I do. And what happens to corporate, public grief? How is the combination of outrage and sorrow ritualized?

Traditional Christian liturgy gives primary place to two forms of prayer: thanksgiving and petition. Even prayers such as confession or invocation are one or the other, or some combination of the two. But experiences of profound suffering, especially unjust suffering, call into question the assumption that these approaches are adequate. For what thanks could be offered that would not deny or devalue the deep suffering that has been endured? And what request can be placed before God which would not suggest that God has not already been beseeched with cries and tears?

Prayers of thanksgiving assume the goodness of God, and prayers of petition assume the omnipotence of God. Experiences of profound, unjust suffering call both of these assumptions into question. The prayer of lament is a third alternative that recognizes the dilemma posed by profound suffering. Judges 11 tells of the ritualized lament of Jephtha's daughter, who is to be sacrificed to fulfill her father's vow. The one favor she asks is permission to go away with her women companions to lament her coming death. Pseudo-Philo, a first-century pseudepigraphal text, provides an imagined version of her lament:

> Hear, you mountains, my lamentation;
> and pay attention, you hills, to the tears of my eyes;
> and be witnesses, you rocks, of the weeping of my soul.
> Behold how I am put to the test!
> But not in vain will my life be taken away.
> May my words go forth in the heavens,
> and my tears be written in the firmament! . . .
> May my virgin companions tell of me in sorrow
> and weep for me through the days.
> You trees, bow down your branches and weep over my
>   youth,
> you beasts of the forest, come and bewail my virginity,
> for my years have been cut off
> and the time of my life cut off in darkness.[21]

A prayer of lament recognizes that terrible harm has been done, and that the harm cannot be undone. No gratitude grows out of such harm, no request can undo it. All that remains is to call the world, both earthly and heavenly, to bear witness to the loss and the harm. Curse, lament, excommunication and exorcism are prayers of refusal: refusal to accept, to yield, to assent to the terror of things-as-they-are.[22]

The feminist reconstruction of prayer builds on the necessary conditions for women and other oppressed people to say no and therefore to say yes. It recognizes the anger and grief of women and the necessity of ritualizing that anger and grief. This reconstruction bears different assumptions about the nature of God and takes new forms.

FINDING OURSELVES IN
FREE-FALL
The Search for a New Language

We must use what we have to invent what we desire.
Adrienne Rich, *What Is Found There*[1]

"Is prayer included in the rituals you plan or participate in?" I asked a group of West coast Christian feminists. The rituals I had participated in had had no traditional prayers directly addressing God. "Of course it is," they said. They enumerated the many forms prayer took: dancing; the use and arrangement of the space; handling of sacred objects, especially natural objects; singing; chanting; drumming; meditating; storytelling. This is a new vocabulary of prayer, I thought.

Rethinking and redoing prayer, like any reconstructive attempt aimed at changing old practices, is difficult and sometimes terrifying work. Yet it can also be exhilarating and liberating, and it is to this work that our search for the transforming *no* and empowering *yes* calls us.

The things that are part of our own lives as women become the building-blocks, the seeds, perhaps the compost of what we need and what we desire: the female body, its desires, cycles, needs, shapes, burdens; our connection with the material and natural world, with things made and things found, with the world as it is and the world as we would recreate it; the sound of our voices, the recognition of our stories, the tears and laughter and rage of our hearts, danced, sung, mourned, shouted and celebrated. Above all, they include that which is forbidden, silenced, rejected, forgotten, despised, ignored, trivialized. They include that which has been assigned to the "Not-A" side of the patriarchal dichotomy, that which has been named as negative, as absence, as unnamed and unnameable. From the landscape of our lives we claim that which is seed and can be planted, that which can be reshaped into building-stone or useful timber. We identify, too, that which cannot be used in its present state, but must be composted into something else, as well as that which is too toxic for compost, and must be removed, exorcised.

Learning to love our *no* is the first, necessary step. The rejection of traditional forms and texts of prayer is the beginning of that *no*, as is the creation of prayers of resistance, of curses and laments. Next is claiming our *yes*, imagining our *yes*, and making our *yes* into reality, creating a noncoercive space where women speak directly and truthfully to God in public, creating an emancipatory vocabulary for that speaking. Feminist liturgy groups find themselves required to invent new ways of praying, developing new vocabulary, new grammar, new syntax for conversation with the Holy One.

Creating Space for Prayer

As Eileen King observes, "as soon as [feminists] enter a space in which they are going to meet, some members of the group will start rearranging the furniture."[2] Patriarchally-defined spaces are not suitable for containing the meanings of feminist gatherings or feminist prayer. Mary Collins argues that this impulse to attend to the space and its arrangement is the impulse of the familiar.[3] Women have traditionally been allowed into this area of ritual work, as sacristans, as members of altar guilds and choirs, as those responsible for creating and caring for the objects used by men. It is not coincidental that this responsibility for the maintenance of material objects duplicates women's cultural roles as caretakers and maintainers of home and physical environment. Nevertheless, as Lesley Northup observes, "Sacred space, far from being an adjunct liturgical consideration, is a central datum in women's ritual experience."[4] Nor do feminist gatherings duplicate the patriarchal patterns of the space they have traditionally been allowed to clean and polish. In place of the patriarchal vertical orientation, feminist groups arrange their space within a horizontal orientation. The authors of a collection of Christian feminist liturgies comment that "the 'sacred' dimension of life is not confined exclusively to designated sanctuary spaces. . . . Worship in a feminist mode blesses and finds blessing in *unexpected* space such as parlor, lounge, or entryway. . . ."[5]

Northup goes on to identify the meanings evoked by this feminist rearrangement of space from hierarchical-vertical arrangements into communal-horizontal circular space. These meanings include de-emphasized leadership, celebration of domesticity and the ordinary, connection with nature, embodiment, and incorporation of secular culture.[6]

This reorientation of space for prayer from the hierarchical to the horizontal recognizes the primacy of the body and of the physical world. As part of a recognition of and attention to bodies and physical objects, it disrupts the A/Not-A dichotomy that separates soul from body and spirit from matter. The preference for horizontal space also enables corporate, communal prayer, thus disrupting hierarchical patterns of authority.

But perhaps fundamental to all of these meanings is the simple act of claiming space. Reorienting a space declares clearly and unambiguously the creation of a domain of power and control. Although traditional Christian piety makes many Christian feminists reluctant to put this into words, claiming power and control of space is implicit in such reorientation. The need for power and control of space for prayer arises out of a knowledge of the suffering women have endured and continue to endure in traditional church spaces. Gail Anderson Ricciuti and Rosemary Catalano Mitchell, describing their feminist liturgies, comment that

> [I]t has been our consistent discipline *not* to hold Women, Word, and Song services in a traditional worship space. We have found that there are many women who can no longer bring themselves to enter church sanctuaries, because of abusive experiences or oppresive memories connected with "church". . . .[7]

The claiming of space by reorienting it declares that this is intended to be safe space for feminist prayer. Within this reclaimed and redefined space women are able to claim the "power to speak," the power to tell our stories, to move our bodies, to sing and cry and shout. This runs contrary to the traditional churches' prayers, which value neither our stories nor our bodies.

Story as Prayer

We know we are without a text, and must discover one.

Carolyn Heilbrun, *Writing a Woman's Life*

The loss of centuries of women's stories is a loss which can never be repaired, only prevented in the future by the telling and re-telling of our stories. Feminist liturgies, however varied they may be, seem always to make room for women to tell their stories. Early feminist groups, with no theological or religious intent at all, developed a system of consciousness-raising that began from the telling of personal stories. Yet the stories we tell are not simply our own; they are also the stories we have been told. As Carolyn Heilbrun observes,

> ... lives do not serve as models; only stories can do that. And it is a hard thing to make up stories to live by. We can only retell and live by the stories we have read or heard. . . . Whatever their form or medium, these stories have formed us all; they are what we must use to make new fictions, new narratives.[8]

Heilbrun argues that it is the lack of narrative plots, our "storylessness," that hinders women. Without a narrative framework, we have no structure for understanding our lives collectively as women on our own terms. We have only patriarchal plots or the refusal of those plots. Biblical plots too have shaped our telling of our own stories: the Fall plot, with woman as Temptress; the Dangerous Woman plot; the Faithful Wife plot; the Mother plot; the Virgin plot. In all of these plots, the woman is secondary to and derivative of the man. Even when the woman (usually the Temptress or Dangerous Woman, sometimes the Mother) demonstrates cunning and initiative, she demonstrates it in spite of—or in reaction against—the restrictions of her life as a woman. Most typically, in patriarchal plots, women's connection with other women is missing or presented negatively. Women appear primarily as rivals for the attention and protection of a man (Ruth being a notable exception).

But this collective story-telling, this creation of a new narrative of our lives, is essential. Heilbrun again:

> I suspect that female narratives will be found where women exchange stories, where they read and talk collectively of ambitions,

and possibilities, and accomplishments. . . . As long as women are isolated one from the other, not allowed to offer other women the most personal accounts of their lives, they will not be part of any narrative of their own.[9]

The inclusion of storytelling in feminist liturgies, then, is a process of creating a female narrative. We overcome our storylessness and the absence of our stories in our religious narrative, and move beyond saying no to the existing plots, to "begin to tell the truth, in groups, to one another," in Heilbrun's words.[10] And out of these new narratives new conversations with the divine and with one another become possible. In the words of Nelle Morton, we "hear one another into speech." Women's stories are sacred, and must be told, to one another as well as to the world. As all sacred stories do, women's stories reveal the workings of God and the absence of God, the presence of holiness and the violation of holiness. As an adult survivor of childhood sexual abuse commented, "Telling is the best revenge." Telling our stories as a process of creating a narrative disrupts the patriarchal story that excludes or misrepresents women.

In many feminist gatherings this storytelling appropriately focuses on participants' stories, or on the reading of contemporary women's stories from around the world. But some Christian feminist groups engage in retelling biblical stories, creating new narratives and disrupting old plots. Ricciuti and Mitchell, for example, describe participants' retelling of the Epiphany text of the Magi:

> We began to muse about whether the journey of the Magi might have been different, and how, had it been a women's story.[11]

As the participants in this Epiphany liturgy discovered, the reconceived story came to a different conclusion than the traditional version.

But in what sense can this storytelling, whether of personal stories or biblical stories, be called prayer? These stories appear to be addressed not to God, as in prayer, but to the gathered community. However, God is commonly understood and experienced in such gatherings not as a hierarchical being "out there" somewhere, but as immanent in many places, most especially in the community itself. Thus telling one's story in the community is telling it to God. But telling one's story also is a means of making

God present to others. Thus the stories become not only our personal stories but God's stories, sacred stories.

Body as Prayer

Feminist liturgies always include some kind of bodily movement: circle dance, gestures, movement from place to place, the handling of sacred objects, anointing of the body, embracing. The embodied character of feminist liturgy and ritual is understood by participants as valuing the female body in defiance of traditional religions' rejection and horror of the female body. The female body as despised and rejected in patriarchal religion is countered by the female human body celebrated in ritual and prayer. Embodied feminist prayer says both *no*—to hatred and fear—and *yes*—to love of female self as body.

However, the female human body is an ambiguous resource. The human body is both text and locus of culture. The body—and how it is dressed, fed, attended to—can be "read" as evidence of the culture and society in which we live. But at the same time culture is embodied in our human bodies, in the multiple, minute, internalized cultural rituals of eating, dressing, and caring for the body's needs. Among other significations, the human body displays and enacts the cultural meanings of gender identity.

The female human body, in contrast to the male human body, is rarely regarded as filling space; women are habituated to fill as little space as possible, to contract our bodies rather that stretching them out.[12] Perhaps for this reason so many women in our culture perceive their bodies as too large, taking up too much space. The female human body is constantly the object of control, either imposed from outside the woman's body, in the form of cultural norms about female behavior and dress, or internalized, in the form of constant self-examination and self-modification through diet, dress, cosmetics, and so on.[13] The creation of unrealistic norms for women's bodies leaves no room for aging, diversity, or physical disability. Moreover, the female human body is culturally and religiously identified with sex: "In Christianity the body scorned, the naked body, is a female body. . . ."[14]

At the same time, the female human body is what we are, what we must learn to love, to cherish and value. It is what we have to pray with. The female human body is the locus of our deepest joys and delights as well as our profoundest pains, betrayals, and alienation. Yet to love ourselves, in our bodiliness, is what we desire, is what we must have to stay alive, physically and spiritually. It is in our bodies, where our breath animates us, that we know the spirit—both our own individual spirits and however we experience the divine spirit.

Feminist embodied prayer is based on the knowledge of these ambiguous female bodies. How is this body knowledge ritualized in prayer? And how can this ritualization take seriously traditional Christianity's rejection of the female human body and its identification with evil, carnality, and sin? How can celebration of the female human body and its cycles resist falling into romantic essentialism that ultimately reinforces unrealistic, negative, and oppressive valuations of women's bodies?

Our body knowledge is a problematic resource to us on two counts. First, the religious mystification and spiritualization of patriarchal definitions of women's bodies (as sexual and erotic or as pure and virginal) create unrealistic and dangerous contexts for our knowing of our own bodies and their meaning. Second, our knowledge of our bodies is distorted by the violence, abuse, and threat with which we live in patriarchal culture; thus even what we know about our bodies and by means of our bodies is distorted by patriarchy and thus to some degree rendered unreliable.

Patriarchal myths about the female human body create impediments for women seeking to pray with and in our bodies:

- The female human body is more closely related to nature, because of its natural cycles.

- Because of their closer connection with nature, women's bodies are more dangerous, *i.e.* chaotic, emotional, volatile.

- Because of their closer connection with nature, women are more intuitive, sensitive to emotions, relationships, children, animals, etc.

- Because of their closer connection with nature, women are both sexual and innocent ("animal"-like).

- Because of their closer connection with nature, women are mysterious.

61

None of these myths has its origin in fact, but in patriarchal fear of and attraction toward female human bodies. In the face of these myths, we must reconstruct our self-knowledge, and assert that we, in fact, know that:

- We are ontologically no closer to nature than any other resident of the earth, human or nonhuman; that we are no more separate from nature than male human beings. That we are, all of us, part of nature, not ranked in a "Great Chain of Being" but part of the same circle of life, all equidistant from the center.

- Attentiveness to the emotions of others is learned, for survival: our own, and others'.

- Being a female human body in a patriarchal world places one at risk of rape, battery, insult, physical or verbal attack, violation, especially by those whom one is supposed to be able to trust, above all by men in positions of authority.

- Success, or even survival, often means being forced either to exploit or to minimize the fact of having a female human body.

- In patriarchal society it is men above all who "have"—in the sense of "possess"—female human bodies; they always assume the right of access to any female human body, and this right also is assumed by law. Catharine MacKinnon observes that "from women's point of view, rape is not prohibited; it is regulated."[15] Patriarchal maleness is defined by access to female bodies.

What does this complex reality of female body knowledge suggest about embodied prayer? Denial of or rejection of the hated female body is required of both women and men in prayer in much of Christian practice. Even drawing attention to one's female body renders the prayer suspect, heretical, obscene. The patriarchal emphasis on purification of the female body after childbirth—(What is it about childbirth that makes the female body impure? The rite is silent on this point.)—becomes "Thanksgiving of a woman after childbirth," then becomes "Thanksgiving for the birth or adoption of a child"; in short the prayer becomes less and less connected to women and to women's bodies.[16]

Women's bodies have not been regarded, in traditional Christian thought or practice, as either appropriate subject matter for prayer, or as appropriate enacters of prayer. "Becoming male" becomes the primary way of access to God in prayer. Exactly how does a female human body "become male"? The classical means for this interesting metaphysical challenge include:

- Renunciation of sexual activity;

- Extreme physical deprivation, especially deprivation of food and cleanliness (two traditionally quintessential female tasks);

- Self-inflicted physical punishment;

- Submission to authority, especially male authority.

A female body becomes male, then, by denying the body's needs and desires, by refusing to listen to the body, by silencing its cries, by hating the female body. Does the male human body have the same needs and desires? Well, in fact it does; and similar strategies have been undertaken by men in preparation for prayer as well. But they are not trying to "become male," to become something they are not, (other than nonphysical). All of the commentators on female holiness note the extraordinary character of the phenomenon, given that it is so much more difficult for women to be holy, due to their natural tendency to be weak and carnal.

Given this complex history, it is necessary to reject some models of embodied prayer, certain ways of ritualizing the female body:

- **Offering or sacrifice:** Sacrifice requires objectification. The objectification of women's bodies is ubiquitous in both church and culture. Prayer that makes our bodies, or the cycles of our bodies, or the products of our bodies separate from our own choices and responsibilities must be rejected. Prayer to God should not require self-sacrifice or denial of desire and pleasure.[17]

- **Submission:** Feminist embodied prayer rejects gestures and postures of submission. Prayer to God should not require acceptance of abuse or abdication of one's own authority, knowledge, will, or voice.

- **Celebration:** The social fact of violence against women's bodies, the religious and spiritual consequences of that violence, and the religious community's collusion in that violence and its consequences make simple celebration of women's bodies problematic. Unqualified celebration of female embodiment adds to the denial of this historic and ingoing violence. Prayer to God should not require denial of women's experience.

Necessary ritualizing of the female body requires recognition of the controverted and highly politicized character of women's bodies in patriarchy. It requires recognition of our ignorance and fear of our own bodies, as well as our desire to value and cherish ourselves. Embodied feminist prayer must include *exploration* and *honor.*

- **Exploration** acknowledges that we are heirs to social and religious traditions and practices that have alienated us from our body-selves. Our embodied prayer thus will necessarily be tentative, experimental. Gestures of dominance and submission are the vocabulary of traditional embodied prayer; feminist embodied prayer experiments with, explores, and discovers gestures and postures of mutuality, equality, and community.

- **Honor** emphasizes the complexity and ambivalence of our own experiences of our bodies. To honor our bodies in embodied prayer means to accept our bodies as they are, not as society or religion would have them be; to learn, slowly, to listen to our bodies' changing desires and needs, and to respect those desires and needs; and to honor and respect other women's differing interpretations of their bodies' desires and needs. Above all it means honoring our bodies as inviolable, as holy, as connected, as ourselves.[18]

Feminist embodied prayer is thus political. The valuing of women's bodies challenges the assumptions of patriarchal society and church, by saying *no* to hatred and fear and alienation and *yes* to discovery and respect. Feminist embodied prayer which explores and honors the female body will be spontaneous, voluntary, and nonregimented.

Objects as Prayer

And with them, or after them, may there not come that even bolder
adventurer—the first geolinguist, who, ignoring the delicate, transient lyrics of the lichen, will read beneath it the still less commu-
nicative, still more passive wholly atemporal, cold, volcanic poetry
of the rocks: each one a word spoken, how long ago, by the earth
itself, in the immense solitude, the immenser community, of space.

Ursula LeGuin, *Buffalo Gals and Other Animal Presences*[19]

Feminist ritual is attentive to the material world, especially
the natural world (rock, leaf, flower, shell, seed, soil, feather) and
the woman-made world (quilt, pot, basket, cloth). The purpose of
this is to connect with and be attentive to (as the man-made
patriarchal world and church are not) the material world of which
we are a part, to counter masculinist religion's disdain for and
suspicion of the material world.

This attentiveness to material objects has its risks. Does it
assume and reinforce patriarchal definitions of female connection
with "nature," or reflect nostalgia for a "women's culture" which
may never have existed? On the other hand, the value of such
attention to the material world is its emphasis on material culture
as created and defined by its participants. Women can and do
create culture; what is critical is that we recognize the political act
inherent in creating culture. It is this recognition that feminist
ritual enacts and enables. By deliberately choosing what objects
will serve as ritual symbols, by determining (to some extent) their
meaning in a feminist ritual context, by participating in other
women's creation of ritual objects, women claim their own ritual-
making and symbol-making power, and at the same time draw
attention to the provisional and man-made nature of patriarchal
religious symbols as well. The religious symbols that we tend to
take for granted, and that have a givenness about them, are
thereby shown to be the result of human choosing and meaning-
making.

The connection between women's bodies and the natural
world is one made both in patriarchal religions (where it often,
as in the case of Christianity, carries a negative association) and
in reconstructions of woman-centered religions (where it most
often carries a positive meaning). The recovery of this connection
between women and nature is often claimed to be necessary to

the salvation of the natural world from the depredations of patriarchal society. As Charlotte Caron notes, "Feminist spirituality suggests that if the world is to survive, women, body, and nature must all be highly valued and that the dualistic mode of thinking and separating must end."[20] But a simple connection between women and nature is problematic, as we have already considered in the context of women's body knowledge.

However, an unromanticized perspective on women and nature, as occupants of the Not-A part of the masculinist dichotomy, as objects of male domination, can disrupt the destructive dichotomy and resist structures of domination. Unfortunately, feminist rituals don't always do this. As Teal Willoughby observes, feminist ritual use of natural symbols, such as water and plants, sometimes replicate patriarchal objectification and instrumentalization of nature.[21] Water is sometimes used for symbolic cleansing, but the water or the earth is made thereby into a repository for human waste, in this case spiritual or emotional waste. Willoughby argues for the creation of ecofeminist ritual that recognizes and ritualizes mutuality between humans and nature, rather than human exploitation of nature.

Feminist ritual use of natural objects, then, must be constructed in full awareness of this human exploitation, being careful not to duplicate this, claiming attentiveness as the appropriate stance toward the natural world. This attentiveness demands, in turn, respect, honor, a willingness to listen to the rock, the shell, the plant, to engage these natural objects on their own terms, rather than as instruments to be manipulated for our own needs. This is how natural objects themselves become prayers: when they are allowed to speak.

The use of symbols drawn from women's traditional domestic work, such as cooking, quilting, weaving, gardening, making of pots and baskets, serves to revalorize work that is routinely devalued and exploited in patriarchal culture and religion. These symbols recognize and honor the work of women's hands, their gifts for creativity, for survival, for creation of beauty in the midst of want, oppression, and suffering. The process of making the ordinary into religious symbols disrupts the patriarchal dichotomy of sacred and profane, and transforms women's work— exploited, enslaved, coerced, unrecognized—into the making of holiness.

Here again, however, it is critical to be aware of this exploitation of women's labor, particularly of poor women, women of color, third world women by white or privileged women. Feminist rituals must avoid perpetuating this exploitation. They must avoid instrumentalizing women's work without regard to the work's creator, the circumstances under which it was created, or the purpose for which it was made. Behind every domestic object created by women's hands lie thwarted gifts, rejected, suppressed, and denied by slavery, misogyny, and colonialism. Attentiveness is necessary here too, as with natural objects, in order to create a ritual context of respect and mutuality. And this context is how woman-made objects become prayers: when their stories and the stories of their makers are told; when the silence that normally surrounds woman-made things is broken; and when the anonymity of the maker is overturned, and her works praise her.

Poetry as Prayer

> A poem can't free us from the struggle for existence, but it can uncover desires and appetites buried under the accumulating emergencies of our lives, the fabricated wants and needs we have urged on us, have accepted as our own.
>
> Adrienne Rich, "Voices from the Air"[22]

Feminist poetry functions in a liturgical way in feminist rituals and liturgies. The imaginative world of the poet is needed for the creation of an alternate world. The language of the poet uses "what we have to invent what we desire," gives names to the desire and to the invention. The imaginative invention, the creative remembering requires the words of the poet, the dreamer, the seer. The freeing of the imagination demands the poet's work. In Audre Lorde's terms, this is poetry as illumination.[23]

Feminist poets insist upon the political meaning and context of their work, its collectivity and sense of responsibility to others. This collectivity, even as the feminist poet insists upon her individuality and particularity, makes feminist poetry particularly relevant to feminist ritual. Adrienne Rich speaks to this balance of individual and collective identity:

> But most often someone writing a poem believes in, depends on, a delicate, vibrating range of difference, that an "I" can become a

"we" without extinguishing others, that a partly common language exists to which strangers can bring their heartbeat, memories, images. A language that itself has learned from the heartbeat, memories, images of strangers.[24]

Feminist poetry, like storytelling, is a mode of breaking the silence of our lives and deepest needs and passions. In Audre Lorde's words, "our silences will not protect us, and the speaking profits us."[25] Feminist poetry helps women uncover our "buried desires and appetites," break the silence about our lives, and find the images and rhythms to tell and retell our stories to one another. This essential discovery of the rhythms of our lives and longings creates a seedbed for the creation of feminist ritual and prayer.

Music as Prayer

Sophia, Creator God,
Let your milk and honey flow.
Sophia, Creator God,
Shower us with your love.

Hilda Kuester, Text of chant for "Blessing over Milk and Honey."[26]

Music plays a central part in feminist prayer. The inspirited body breathes, vibrates, and sings. The female voice claims the power to sing, to shout, to keen, to laugh. In making music we use our body, we claim our voice, we find and create a women's musical culture.

Feminist liturgy groups show a preference for communal song over solo, for chant over elaborate polyphony, for drum, guitar, bells, and rattles over piano and organ. To claim our own musical voice, we desire to hear as many different voices as possible. To engage as many participants in making music as possible, we desire to make our music simple.

But this does not happen without struggle. The power of music has always been recognized by the church, but that power has also long been mistrusted. On the one hand, early Christian leaders regarded singing as an indispensible part of worship of God; on the other hand, they feared its emotional, seductive, and physical quality. Especially they rejected the use of musical instruments, perhaps because instrumental music lacks verbal content and thus is more difficult to interpret and control. Moreover, the rejection of instrumental music in early Christian music had the advantage of distinguishing Christians from Jews and pagans. Monophony, singing in unison, became the model of Christian song, representing as it did the univocality of the church.[27]

That this univocality was deeply gendered is shown in two ways. First, the rhetorical structure of ancient theory about music reflects patriarchal standards. Clement of Alexandria speaks of the unity that is the goal of Christian music:

> We want to strive so that we, the many, may be brought together into one love, according to the union of the essential unity. . . . The union of many, which the divine harmony has called forth out of a medley of sounds and division, becomes one symphony, following the one leader of the choir and teacher, the Word, resting in that same truth and crying out: "Abba, Father."

This pure music—unison only, and unaccompanied by instruments—follows the "Fatherly will of God." This distinguishes it from non-Christian ("Not-A") music, which is intemperate:

> . . . we shall keep far from our virile minds all liquid harmonies which by modulating tones lead to a dangerous art which trains to effeminacy and languor.[28]

The "virile mind," that is, the true Christian mind, avoids the female, "liquid" music that leads to "effeminacy": A avoids contamination by Not-A; manhood is protected from watery femaleness. Centuries later this same argument appears in a papal document:

> A person who is intrinsically sensuous will delight in hearing these indecent melodies, and one who listens to them frequently will be weakened thereby and lose his virility of soul.[29]

Given this thoroughgoing masculinism in musical theory, it is hardly surprising to add that the practice of women's singing in Christian worship was controverted, and consistently suppressed, forbidden, restricted, or controlled. Women were allowed to sing along with men, but not to sing alone in women's choirs; women's voices were seductive and dangerously sensuous. Women were advised to move their lips, but make no sound; to only whisper the words of the hymn; to confine their singing to the privacy of their chamber.[30] This silencing of women's voices is part of our heritage, as is the masculinization of the Christian identity. Thus the singing of women in feminist liturgy groups, and the use of musical instruments—especially despised ones such as drums and bells—are acts of defiance and resistance.

But even when this history is not known, or recognized only in faint echo, there are other reasons for the interest in the use of music in feminist ritual. As a form of prayer, music is powerful, and powerfully embodied. As a form of ritual, music exists only in the present and thus enables simultaneous ritual action. But, above all, music is physical; it is this very physicality that surely alarmed Clement of Alexandria and other patristic writers. This quality of music is described by Walter Ong as follows:

> It makes interiors known as interiors without the necessity of physical invasion (as would be true of touch).[31]

Women know what it is to be physically invaded; women's bodies are culturally regarded as invadable. A noninvasive recognition of interiority—such as is accomplished through music—is a very good definition of feminist prayer.

BY WHOSE POWER?
The Problem of Divine
Authority for Feminist Prayer

> God is not Our Father at all. My image of him now is of something
> huge, hard, inexorable, faceless and moving forward as if on tracks.
> God is a sort of engine.
>
> Margaret Atwood, *Cat's Eye*[1]

The subject of the feminist reconstruction of our understanding of God is too vast to be dealt with in one chapter. In any
case, we are not concerned with the systematic or constructive
theological project, but with the practical questions of to whom
do we pray, and how? All praying presumes meeting. Who is this
One with whom we meet and desire to communicate? What
elements of traditional public prayer enable that meeting and that
communication, and what elements disrupt it? What do women
desire to say to the One to whom we pray, and how do we wish
to construct the conversation? Or is "conversation" itself too
limiting a term, too anthropocentric? The God of Margaret Atwood's character Elaine, as quoted above, is not anthropomorphic at all, but mechanical and impersonal. What sort of authority
and power does the God to whom we pray exercise?

Beginning with these questions about prayer as meeting with
and discourse with God, rather than the questions of systematic
theology as discourse about God, the central issue is one of power.
To paraphrase Adrienne Rich, with whom do we believe God's lot
is cast? What kind of authority do we believe God to have, and
how does that power express itself? The act of praying raises the
relational question with an urgency that need not apply in con-
siderations of language or discourse about God. The question

about God for feminist prayer is, then, is God trustworthy? Does God care about women? Certainly these questions raise issues of language and symbol; but in the context of encounter and meeting. Can we trust God enough to have a conversation? What are the terms of that conversation, and who decides?

The Authority of God in Contemporary Liturgical Prayers

Conventional wisdom suggests that of course God is authoritative; otherwise why bother to pray? The assumption that God is at the same time both all-powerful and inscrutable is commonplace, and is articulated most clearly in times of crisis or disaster: God has surely spared us for some purpose, destroyed them for some reason, but the reasons and purposes are unavailable to us. If we are spared, we are blessed; if we are not spared, we are cursed. We cannot bear to consider that tragedies occur without meaning. Yet in claiming some hidden divine reason for terrible suffering, we create an interpretation which attributes to God a certain capriciousness. God's omnipotence is in conflict with God's goodness.

Nevertheless, contemporary public prayers generally express confidence in both God's goodness and God's power. The dominant notes are thanksgiving, confession (or request for pardon), and petition. Petitions are usually rather general and mild; that is, God is not often importuned in published corporate prayers. Typical requests, embedded in opening prayers, collects, and the like, include requests that God "enlighten our path," "open our hearts and minds," "bless us with your wisdom," in addition to requests for pardon.[2] Occasionally there are requests for comfort, healing, or protection. Most material requests appear in intercessory prayers, which in published liturgies are found in the "prayers of the people." For example the *Book of Common Prayer* of the Episcopal Church (USA) includes petitions for "seasonable weather, and for an abundance of the fruits of the earth . . . [and] . . . for deliverance from all danger, violence, oppression, and degradation."[3]

The relationship between God and those praying reflected in these prayers is congenial and benign. The tone is respectful and polite, even in prayers requesting pardon for our sins, which

72

generally appear to assume that God will forgive us. Petitions are usually nonurgent in tone, as perhaps might be expected in composed general petitions; urgent requests would be occasional and local; some forms for intercession allow for such expressions.[4]

This benign and moderate tone appears to leave no room for expressions of outrage, grief, or lament. Women survivors of violence and abuse and those who are aware of the extent of such suffering thus often feel like illegitimate worshipers in a traditional mainstream Christian worship service. Expressions of confidence in God's goodness and faith in God's power to protect and care for us ring hollow indeed. Where is this benign God when a child is being raped by her father? Where is this powerful God when a woman is beaten or shot to death by her male partner? Where is this compassionate God when women in non-Western countries are systematically denied adequate food, health care, social services, and education available to men?

The anguish of these questions is increased by the conventional male language used to address God. Thus God appears not only to be indifferent to women's suffering, but also positively identified with male persons who are most often women's abusers.

The church's preference for a prayer discourse which is unitary, both theologically and expressively, has already been argued. This unitary model is based on certain patriarchal conventions and assumptions about God and our relationship with God that are rarely questioned and in fact leave no room for questions.

The Conventions of Traditional Christian Liturgical Prayer

Almighty God,
to you all hearts are open, all desires known,
and from you no secrets are hidden.
Cleanse the thoughts of our hearts
by the inspiration of your Holy Spirit,
that we may perfectly love you,
and worthily magnify your holy name,
through Christ our Lord.

Book of Common Prayer

Borrowing heavily from the protocols of the ancient public world for dealing with strict class systems and powerful rulers, traditions of Christian prayer developed a verbal and gestural vocabulary that makes certain assumptions and claims about the One we address in prayer.

A primary assumption is that God is male, or God is best addressed by male-identified titles; some argue that certain male-identified titles reveal such fundamental aspects of God's nature that to alter them at all is to pray to another God.[5] A milder but not substantively different view is that God is male but has certain (male-defined) feminine characteristics, especially nonthreatening ones, like nurturing, relational attributes, etc.[6] Anything suggesting femaleness is thus subsumed under the more general category of divine maleness. Maleness is A. Everything else is Not-A. Even though classical theological reflection has insisted that God is not male in the sense of having a male body, all males known to us have male bodies, and the consequence of this assumption about God's male identity is to value (even deify) the male body, while devaluing (even demonizing) the female body.

God is andromorphized, that is, addressed in terms most often used to refer to male, powerful human beings. A sharp distinction is made between God's manlike characteristics, and so-called nature, which is subject to God's (and man's) control. Human beings are A; everything else, including nonhuman animals, plants, rivers and seas, rocks and stones, are Not-A. Female human beings actually occupy an anomalous role in this scheme, being on the one hand human (according to some writers) but on the other hand dangerously close to the chaotic, uncontrollable "nature." Aristotle's scientific conclusion that the conception of female humans was the result of some atmospheric disturbance, such as "a warm south wind," offers a particularly tidy example of this thinking, and a convenient solution to the theoretical problem, in patriarchal thinking, of the existence of female human beings. The female human body thus appears as much more of a spiritual problem than the male, and seems closer to animal bodies and to the natural world in general. Like the bodies of nonhuman animals and the "natural" world, women's bodies are regarded as violable.

God is identified with and upholds patriarchal values: dominance, hierarchical power, absolute authority. This too is sometimes softened but not changed by the argument that the one who is almighty is also the vulnerable one. But this is a deceptive romanticization of vulnerability. One who is almighty may choose to become vulnerable, but the truly vulnerable, the poor, the helpless, the oppressed, are forced to be vulnerable and have no choice to be mighty. Theories of dominance and submission, especially when attached to divine images, reinforce and legitimate male dominance of women, nonhuman animals, and "nature."

Implicit in these patriarchal models of God is the assumption of divine and human hierarchy. God is "above" in the social sense (indicated by the use of social titles like "King" and "Lord") and in the sense of superior power ("Almighty"). These assumptions about God's nature and human nature affect the relationship between God and those who pray, and are expressed in both the content and the conventions of traditional prayer.

Those who pray approach God as supplicants before an absolute monarch/patriarchal father, who is distant from and completely other than the supplicants. God is addressed by titles which express respect for patriarchal authority and power, whether human or divine: Almighty, Eternal, Lord, Father, King.

The supplicants have no right to question the monarch/father God; he not only knows best, he knows all. By comparison, we are hopelessly ignorant: "Accept and fulfill our petitions, not as we ask in our ignorance, nor as we deserve in our sinfulness, but as you know and love us in your Son Jesus Christ our Lord."[7]

Obedience to and self-abasement before the monarch/father is prerequisite to making any requests. "We do not presume to come to this thy table, O merciful Lord, trusting in our own righteousness, but in thy manifold and great mercies. We are not worthy so much as to gather up the crumbs under thy table." This God's omniscience makes prayer logically problematic, a fact which many traditional prayers recognize openly: "you know our needs before we ask." The implication is, however, that we have to name our needs or sins even though God already knows them, for our own good. Essential to this confession is the declaration of God's superiority and omniscience.

Because of the otherness of God, purity is also prerequisite; the female body is a primary locus of pollution, and thus references to women's bodies or bodily functions in prayer language are impure and taboo. A recent example of this taboo is the conservative reaction to a prayer at the much-maligned Minneapolis meeting celebrating the ecumenical decade in solidarity with women. The prayer in question gave thanks to God for women's bodies and named women's bodies as holy. This was regarded by these critics as at best in poor taste, at worst blasphemous. In some periods of history and in some contemporary traditions, women's ability to pray rightly (*i.e.*, purely) is doubtful or even rejected out-of-hand.

God is all-seeing and all-knowing; it is not possible to escape or hide from the father/monarch. "From you no secrets are hidden." We are assumed to be continually under God's constant surveillance, whether benign or ominous. Anne Marie Hunter has argued, based on her experience as an advocate for battered women, that the varied stories of women that she heard had the common theme of the controlling male gaze. Following Michel Foucault's analysis of surveillance of prisoners, she notes first the generalized surveillance of women by men. Women are defined as in need of such surveillance:

> Depending on the race, class, sexual orientation, or age of any particular woman, it may be claimed that she is helpless and needs help, out of control and needs control, dependent and needs support, childish and needs supervision, property and needs policing, or strong and independent and needs "cutting down to size."[8]

The intrusive and abusive surveillance reported by battered women thus can be seen as an extreme form of social control experienced to some degree by all women in patriarchal society. As indicated by the "Collect for Purity" quoted above, Christian prayer often emphasizes God's omniscience, represented by the "all-seeing eye" of God. As Hunter notes, God's pervasive gaze may in some circumstances be perceived as benign, even comforting. The God of Exodus sees the people's suffering and oppression and responds to it. Intercessory prayers frequently invoke God's understanding of human need and human limitations:

> Gracious God, because we are not strong enough to pray as we should, you provide Jesus Christ and the Holy Spirit to intercede for us in power.[9]

The answer to our weakness, in this prayer, is God's power, as God's knowledge is the remedy for our ignorance in the following:

> . . . . Accept and fulfill our petitions, we pray, not as we ask in our ignorance, nor as we deserve in our sinfulness, but as you know and love us in Jesus Christ our Lord.[10]

As this prayer suggests, references to God's knowledge of us in Christian prayer discourse is just as likely to carry a vaguely threatening tone, as it also does in the "Collect for Purity." Originally the priests' prayer of preparation before the Mass, the "Collect for Purity" assumes the necessity of purity for right celebration of the ritual, as well as the unlikelihood that the priests are sufficiently self-aware to know how sinful they might be. Thus the attribution of omniscience to God is intended as a defense in requesting cleansing and purification. The request for purification implies that to celebrate the Mass impurely would be dangerous or harmful, especially for the celebrant. Just as impurity is tied to ignorance in the Collect for Purity, ignorance is tied to sinfulness in the prayer quoted above. God knows all; by contrast, we know nothing, and our ignorance is often depicted as sinful or polluting.

Hunter argues that the God of the Bible is depicted as exercizing this panoptic gaze in ways that are "eerily familiar" to one who knows the stories of battered women. These biblical images replicate and echo the abusive and intrusive controlling gaze of the batterer, who is jealous, judgmental, and unrelenting in pursuing and controlling the woman. Thus this God, Hunter argues, "does not see or know from women's point of view." Instead, this all-seeing God transcends the surveillance of the batterer, observing the woman's innermost thoughts and feelings, which she may have learned to conceal from her violent partner:

> This all-seeing God extends the normative male gaze into the most private recesses of women's lives, into those moments of solitude that have yet to be reached by any human eye. Thus, this God deepens, and is implicated in, the profound alienation, objectification, and self-doubt that debilitate all women.[11]

These characteristics assigned to God in patriarchal discourse replicate the characteristics of an abusive father as perceived by an abused child: the self-abasement, the assumption of unquestioned authority, the apparent omniscience, the rejection of the polluting female body. One needs to add only the threat of punishment to complete the picture.

Traditional prayer language also includes certain structural and nonverbal conventions which add to and confirm this patriarchal and hierarchical pattern. The structural pattern which always emphasizes God's absolute authority (Almighty, everlasting God), or which always includes declarations of the unworthiness of the worshipers (we your unworthy servants) exemplify this pattern. Further, some of the conventional postures of prayer, especially the posture of head bowed and eyes closed (to say nothing of prostrations), duplicates the posture of submission before an absolute monarch. Bowing and kneeling have their roots and echoes in the power relationships between master and servant or slave. To bow or prostrate one's self is to make one's self completely physically vulnerable, unable to defend one's self. To bow the head is to bare the neck, inviting the ruler before whom one bows to cut off one's head if it pleases him to do so.

Immediately one can think of exceptions to these characteristics. Some forms of prayer, such as imprecation and lament, and postures such as standing, forms of address for God which are less hierarchical, all stand in sharp contradiction to the patterns I have indicated. Patriarchal discourse only strives for unity; these and other examples may be considered part of the suppressed voices, coming through the fissures.

Immediately too comes the objection that submission to God is of an entirely different order than submission to human authority, and indeed may be seen (and has been seen) as directly subversive to all human authority. This is true. It is also true that submission to God has been conveniently tied to the use of human titles of power for God (Master, King, Lord, Father) to suggest—no, let's not be euphemistic—to enforce the submission of persons with little or no power to persons with great power.

> Wives, be subject to your husbands, as you are to the Lord. . . . Slaves, obey your earthly masters with fear and trembling, in singleness of heart, as you obey Christ; not only while being watched, and in order to please them, but as slaves of Christ, doing the will of God from the heart. (Ephesians 5:22, 6:5-6)

The fact that the same discourse can be used in diametrically opposed ways draws attention to a difference in voice. The *patriarchal* reading of submission to God is that it supports submission to patriarchal authority. An alternative reading, seen through the fissures in patriarchal discourse, is that submission to God subverts patriarchal authority. Nevertheless, there is a feminist suspicion of submission language which makes us doubt the ultimate subversiveness of this language, particularly when equally strong traditions connect divine authority with certain forms of human, especially male, authority.

How then does a woman pray to such a God? What is the content of her address? How does she resist or reject the protocols of submission and self-abasement, and how does she create new protocols that value her own authority and her own voice? Or is prayer to such a God possible or useful? Must some alternative image of God be discovered? Does feminist prayer need to engage the patriarchal God, or does it need to claim a feminist face of God?

Is God an Abuser?

This will be my chant,
where were you when I needed you?

"Beth's Psalm"[12]

Where God is expected to be all-powerful (as in all traditional Christian prayer), God's failure to come to the aid of the oppressed, of the raped, of the battered, of the abused, is experienced as the worst kind of betrayal. A young woman who was raped at the age of sixteen comments on Psalm 27:

"I have asked but one thing of the Lord"—that he keep his promises! If you are my protector, then protect me. If you cannot protect me, at least tell me so. Don't pretend you can conceal me, protect me, or shield me. Don't pretend to be a rock or a shepherd. Don't pretend to have a sukka.

"'I have asked one thing of the Lord'—please heal me, and please don't let that ever happen to anyone else again. On the day of evil, I was not concealed in a sukka, whatever that is. . . . I was an open target. I was a lamb, and the shepherd was asleep."[13]

Biblical and liturgical texts which emphasize God's providential care are challenged by these voices. Prayer to this God—who is indifferent or asleep—becomes an accusation: "Where were you when I needed you?"[14] God is not accused of being a direct cause of the suffering and abuse, but God is accused of failing in God's promises of faithful care. By this failure, God is complicit in the violence, an accessory, if you will.

Jewish theologian David Blumenthal takes a slightly different approach to the problem of God's complicity in the evil in the world, particularly the Holocaust and child abuse. Considering scriptural texts as well as the horrors of these events, he concludes that God is not merely complicit, but actually guilty. God is an abusing God, he argues, who not only allows but engages in violence and abuse. The genocide of the Jewish people in the Holocaust and the destruction of human well-being by child abuse are both caused by and allowed to happen by God, not for any good purpose, but because abusiveness is an atttribute of God, "but not always":

> In this mode, God allows the innocent to suffer greatly. In this mode, God "caused" the holocaust, or allowed it to happen.[15]

He concludes that because God is at times abusive, God's victims must approach God as they would an abuser: with clarity about our own innocence and God's guilt, with rage and grief, and with distrust of God. He also argues that all of these approaches are necessary because rejection of God is not possible. Not possible because God is creator/parent, and absolute rejection of parents is impossible; the tie that exists cannot be denied, even when the relationship can be rejected. And not possible because he assumes that alongside the experience of betrayal by God there are also experiences of goodness that may be named as experiences of God. Finally, God cannot be rejected because to do theology is to claim a religious tradition as home.

Blumenthal's arguments against rejection of God can be challenged on feminist grounds, however. God is not only creator/parent, but also lover/spouse. If the blood ties of the parental relationship cannot be denied (although this too seems highly debatable), the voluntary relationship of lovers can. His parental model of God seems heavily dependent on a patriarchal model of parenthood in which the child is the property of the father. Further, the idea of a religious tradition as one's home raises feminist critiques of the patriarchal family and calls forth awareness of the prevalence of violence against women and children in the home. The image of the home is hardly a friendly one for women. Moreover, feminist theologians have observed the similarity between the church and the home/family as patriarchal institutions. Male-dominated religious traditions like Christianity (and Judaism) are not and have not been hospitable to women; loyalty to religious traditions that are hostile to one's well-being is hardly healthy or appropriate.

However, Blumenthal's argument that God cannot be utterly rejected because it would not be true to our contrary experiences with the goodness of God is consistent with much of feminist theological thought. Feminist theologians have generally insisted that God supports and endorses women's struggle for survival and dignity. God is good in spite of church and religious institutions. In some cases, this perception of God as good and caring reflects indebtedness to liberation theologians, for whom God is not the abuser/oppressor (sinful human beings or sinful humanly designed social structures are) but is rather the liberator, always on the side of the oppressed. In contrast to Blumenthal's notion, which preserves God's power at the expense of God's justice, liberation theologians emphasize God's justice, but at the apparent cost of God's power. (A God who is both powerful and just would not allow oppression or abuse.) In either case, however, justice is not done, and women and children are not protected or saved from destruction, and God's trustworthiness and reliability are questionable. And more to our point, in either case, one must ask, what is the point in praying to a God who is either unable or unwilling to help?

Another option, that of the God who suffers with us, proposed by some theologians, leaves the question of prayer even more in doubt. A friend who was raped commented, "It was reassuring to learn from a rape crisis support group that I was not the only woman ever to be raped; but knowing that other women had been raped did not make me feel better, or safer." As Joanne Carlson Brown and Rebecca Parker note,

> The identification in Suffering God theology of solidarity with redemption should be questioned. Bearing the burden with another does not take the burden away. Sympathetic companionship makes suffering more bearable, but the friendship between

slaves, for example, does not stop the master from wielding the lash.[16]

And what of prayer to the Suffering God? It hardly makes sense to ask for or expect help from a God who suffers. But it could be argued that while friendship between slaves does not stop the master from wielding the lash, political organizing among slaves could very well generate (and has indeed generated) slave revolts that have in fact removed the lash from the master's hand. Is such a model of political solidarity and organizing useful in rethinking prayer?

The decision not to pray is one sometimes made by religious people in the face of devastating suffering. An adult survivor of child abuse comments,

> For now, I have nothing to say to God because, like all abused children, I expect no response that will help. . . . Just as I have deliberately simplified my world for two years by interacting emotionally with very few people, so too have I withdrawn from God. He offers no comfort, only stress and complication.[17]

Having nothing to say to God, refusing to maintain the relationship established in prayer, is a legitimate response to abuse, whether the abuser is God or another person. It is, as this woman notes, a form of self-care, necessary to the process of recovery from trauma.

Another way of understanding God's apparent brutality is hardly orthodox (but seeing God as an abuser is hardly orthodox either) but moves beyond seeing God in anthropomorphic or andromorphic ways. By taking the human animal as a metaphor for understanding and relating to God, perhaps we create more problems for ourselves than we resolve. Perhaps a more useful model is of God as wild (i.e., untamed) nonhuman creature. Taking human-animal relations as a model does several things at once. It disrupts hierarchical notions of power, particularly male-dominated "chain of being" assumptions about "higher" and "lower" organisms. It reclaims numinosity by relocating "otherness" and "difference" in a nondichotomous context. It crosses the man-made distance between human and nonhuman animals by assuming metaphorical similarity between human and nonhuman animals. And it builds on existing and imagined relationships with nonhuman animals that often involve pleasure, fear, awe, anger. God seen as bear, or wolf, or eagle, and therefore as inherently dangerous to humans, decenters our humanocentric universe, suggesting that perhaps divine power is not exclusively or even primarily concerned with us. It may also problemize human exploitation of (i.e. hunting, factory-farming, eating, wearing) nonhuman animals.[18] The problem of God's brutality takes on different meaning when God is analogized as an animal; even a domesticated animal may inadvertently do injury to a human; even more do we anticipate the possibility of injury when dealing with "wild" animals. This view may mitigate rage and blame of God, and may also promote wariness and self-protection in approaching God.

Given women's dangerous knowledge of violence and abuse and oppression, what forms of prayer are possible, what forms are necessary?

The Relocation of Power in Feminist Prayer

The loving eye does not prohibit a woman's experiencing the world directly, does not force her to experience it by way of the interested interpretations of the seer in whose visual field she moves. In this situation, she can experience directly in her bones the contingent character of her relations to all others and to Nature.

Marilyn Frye, The Politics of Reality: Essays in Feminist Theory[19]

Feminist perspectives are suspicious of power and its uses; it has too often been and still is used against women and others to oppress, to harm, to harass, to erase. At the same time, women need and desire power; to claim it for our own, to learn to use it for our own well-being, for the well-being of others, for the well-being of the world. The problem with conventional public prayer is that it locates all beneficent power in God, presumes a limited amount of power, makes the use of power by women problematic, sinful, demonic. Feminist prayer therefore must begin by challenging these assumptions, beginning with the assumption that only God uses power beneficently.

Feminist prayer, which begins with the dangerous knowledge of women's bodies, of women's lives, dares to address the divine in a different voice. The male voice of traditional public prayer cannot carry this knowledge; it is a vehicle that is entirely the wrong shape, the shape of dominance and submission, of hierarchical power, of indifference to suffering. The form of address, the posture of the knowing body, changes the perception of the one addressed in prayer. The knowing feminist pray-er knows God differently.

What does she know? She knows ambivalence. God is not simple, unitary, perhaps not even one. God has not only many names, but many faces. If God is seen in the people and world around us as well as in the words of Scripture, liturgy, and tradition, then God is multiple and complex. Some of God's faces are judgmental, jealous, abusive, uncaring. God is seen in this case in the faces of violent, abusive men, indifferent people, judgmental religious leaders, and in the grinding oppression of impersonal social systems that claim divine authority. This God we cannot love; to offer this God worship would be the worst kind of denial of our well-being. This God's injustice demands rejection, accusation. But God's face is also seen in the compassionate friend, the angry advocate, the tireless worker for justice; in these places we see God as compassionate, active, engaged in the struggle with us. This face of God is loved and praised; this face of God is worthy of worship. The problem, of course, is to deal constructively with these apparent contradictions in God and in our relationship with God. Multiple faces demand multiple responses.

Our anger at our betrayal by God's injustice and unfaithfulness demands varied expression, depending upon particular contexts and experiences. Among the options must be silence, accusation, and waiting. Silence recognizes that distrust is, in Blumenthal's words, "a proper religious affection."[20] To refuse to address God directly, as suggested above, may be the action demanded by appropriate self-care. Accusation names God as culpable for one's suffering, for women's suffering, and calls God to account and to repentance. Waiting means to give God the opportunity to confess, to acknowledge the harm done and to repent of it. This amounts to a refusal to accept the violent face of God, as is. As a Dutch feminist litany puts it, "You are not my God, Father-God, when [you support or allow injustice]. . . ."[21]

Feminist theology and prayer have intentionally developed images of God as female, not only to counter conventional views of God as male, but also to revalue female power, body, and experience.[22] At the same time, feminist prayer has often deemphasized the authority of God in favor of divine goodness. Perhaps this preference for goodness is influenced by rejection of traditional forms of authority, which have been male-identified and most often arrayed against women. Perhaps the emphasis on divine goodness stems from attempts to address God in female human terms in a cultural religious context in which the preferred female models are good without having authority. Are divine goodness and authority compatible? Are female goodness and authority imaginable? A related problem with female God-language is noted by Carol J. Adams:

> References to femaleness no matter how metaphorical (and God-language is metaphorical to the core) are experienced as references to female bodies, female bodies that are seen as sexually available through the lens of male dominance. As a result, women's bodies carry so much baggage regarding carnality that imputing divinity to femaleness becomes difficult and arouses great resistance.[23]

The identification of female body with sex is deeply embedded not only in culture but in the psyches of all of us, men and women alike. No one who has begun to address God/Goddess as female has avoided learning this hard fact. The resistance comes not only from external patriarchal authority but also from within. Nevertheless, seeing divinity as female, embodied, powerful and good is possible, and may indeed be a necessary spiritual discipline for the creation of feminist prayer. But this discipline cannot afford to deny the male sexualization of women's bodies, male domination and control of women's bodies, or male violence against and abuse of women's bodies. Prayer to God as Goddess resists the temptation to romanticize women or reinscribe patriarchal models of the "feminine divine" by confronting this systematic devaluing of women's bodies. What is needed is not the "feminine divine" but the "divine feminist."

A prominent feminist model of relationship is sisterhood. Even when problemized by recognition of horizontal violence among women and by participation of privileged white women in oppression of women of color, sisterhood remains the hope of feminist consciousness and the goal of feminist strategies. Elisabeth Schüssler Fiorenza notes,

If feminist theologies relinquish the claim that their critiques and insights have universal validity, they are in danger of feeding into postcolonial attempts at crisis management that operate through the particularization, fragmentation, and regionalization of the disenfranchised and oppressed.[24]

The claim that oppression of women in patriarchal culture and church is shared by all women, even as our particular existences give that oppression particular shapes, is central to the creation of solidarity among women. To use religious language, we recognize that sisterhood is an eschatological hope, toward which we struggle and move. This hope has at times been expressed in prayer addressed to God as Sister. The expectation that God shares both our struggles and our hopes risks the problems of a powerless God identified in the foregoing discussion. On the other hand, it also is faithful to the experience of many women that God is known in our experience primarily in the lives of beloved women. Although we might expect this conversation to be more intimate, duplicating the best of what Janice Raymond calls "gyn/affection," friendship among women, it is also likely to be marked at times with anger. For it is in the nature of patriarchal reality that women are pitted against women, that strategies of "postcolonial crisis management" have fostered and continue to foster divisions among us that are real and painful.

Related to the model of God as Sister is the experience of God as diverse, complex, and representing multiple points of view, rather than a panoptic view. Thus God is not the ultimate source of power and knowledge; God's knowledge is partial and fragmented, and God's power is shared. Moreover, in this model the sharing of power is mutual. God shares God's power and knowledge with us; we share our power and knowledge with God. Knowledge of the extent of violence against women and children, and knowledge of the interlocking structures of oppression that multiply suffering for those located at the bottom of the patriarchal pyramid, challenges assumptions about the patriarchal uses of power. Hierarchical power, of which God is the primary wielder, is radically decentered and shown to be inimicable to the well-being of women and other oppressed people. Exclusive control over knowledge—a kind of power—is radically dismantled in this model. Instead of being a way of constantly asking God for favors and assuming the posture of supplicants before absolute knowledge and power, prayer thus becomes conversation in the truest sense and meeting in the mutual sense. Admittedly this model limits God far more dramatically than conventional theology has allowed. But it is a realistic response to feminist knowledge about the dangers of concentrated power. Perhaps this is something women and other oppressed people know that God does not know, but needs to know.

A Literary Post-Script

The epigraph at the beginning of this chapter quotes from Margaret Atwood's novel, *Cat's Eye*. The text quoted is in the mind of the main character, the child Elaine Risley. It is her theological conclusion after suffering all manner of psychological abuse from a group of female classmates, one in particular. In a fruitless attempt to placate this tormenting girl, Elaine attends church and Sunday School with her and her family, and memorizes Bible verses and religious songs. When her pious efforts do not redeem her from her tormentor, she concludes that God is indifferent, machinelike. (On Sunday afternoons, the family with whom Elaine goes to church always drives out to the railroad tracks to watch trains come in.) However, it would be unfair not to follow Elaine's spiritual development further. In rebellion, she not only rejects God the Father, but discovers the Virgin Mary. In the Protestant world in which she lives, her interest is illegitimate, yet she finds that there is something comforting in the image of the woman in the blue robe. After discovering this image, Elaine begins "to do something dangerous, rebellious, perhaps even blasphemous." Unable to pray to the impersonal, punishing God, she decides to pray to the Virgin Mary:

> I try to think what I would tell her. But she knows already: she knows how unhappy I am.
> I pray harder and harder. My prayers are wordless, defiant, dry-eyed, desperate, without hope.[25]

She sees in her inner eye a vision of the Sacred Heart of Mary. Later, when she almost freezes to death as a result of the malicious treatment of the girls, she sees a redemptive vision of the Virgin telling her, "You can go home now. It will be all right. Go home."

87

The redemptive woman on the bridge, comforting and reassuring, saving her life, is her adult self.

From her desperate acquisition of the trappings of Protestant religion the child Elaine hopes to save herself from her emotional torment. But Father-God is unable to save her. Instead, a found image of the Virgin of the Seven Sorrows opens a door to her, offers the image of a divine redemptive woman who also knows sorrow, and knows that the child Elaine is unhappy. In Elaine's moment of extreme suffering and danger, it is this image that saves her: the image that is in her already, that is herself, her future. She found deliverance in herself.

IN WHOSE NAME?
The Problem of Jesus
for Feminist Prayer

He said to them, "But who do you say that I am?"
> Matthew 16:15

Begotten of the Father eternally as to Divinity, born of the Virgin
Theotokos, temporally as to humanity.
> The Council of Chalcedon

My grandmother's Christ was one she could talk to about the daily
struggles of being poor, Black, and female. . . . But most importantly, it is in the face of my grandmother, as she struggled to
sustain herself and her family, that I truly see Christ.
> Kelly Brown Douglas, *The Black Christ*[1]

As in the previous chapter on God, this chapter on Jesus
cannot hope to examine every aspect of feminist reconsiderations
of the significance of Jesus for Christian theology and identity.
Rather, we must focus on the relationship of prayer to the symbol
of Jesus within Christian liturgical discourse. Traditional Christian prayer is offered "in the name of Jesus." What does this
signify for women who pray? How have feminist liturgy groups
understood praying "in the name of Jesus"? How does the symbol
of Jesus function to reinforce patriarchal relations and how does
it function to disrupt and reorder those relations?

Clearly, as in the case of prayer to God, a central issue in
feminist prayer "in the name of Jesus" is the issue of power. In
conventional prayer discourse, the name of Jesus is invoked
precisely because it is interpreted as being powerful. It is also
invoked in order to reestablish the orthodoxy of the prayer, so its

power includes the power of conformity and univocality. Moreover, even more intensively than in prayer to God, the issue of maleness and masculinity comes to the fore in the invocation of Jesus' name. The male identity and masculine authority of Jesus have been invoked throughout Christian history to restrict women's exercise of religious authority. Furthermore, the traditional interpretations of Jesus' life and death, particularly in terms of their meaning for us, create problems. The meaning of Jesus' life and death for us is normally called salvation or redemption. Within patriarchal discourse, salvation has been interpreted in terms that valorize and glorify Jesus' suffering and death. Feminist theologians have struggled to reinterpret these events in ways that are not harmful to women and other oppressed people.

Doctrinal statements on the nature of Jesus Christ speak of his identity in gendered language that reflects the patriarchal discourse of the ancient imperial world. Pietistic approaches to Jesus in prayer romanticize his character in terms that replicate contemporary gendered relationships, emphasizing the necessity of a "personal relationship" with a masculine Lord and Savior. Traditional prayer overwhelmingly emphasizes Jesus' sacrificial and self-giving love for humanity. But emerging feminist voices identify Jesus neither with imperial power nor with romantic plots, but with the struggle of women and other oppressed people for survival and dignity. Similarly, feminist prayer struggles with the traditional interpretation of Jesus, in light of the use of Jesus' maleness against the very act of women's praying. What strategies are used in feminist prayers to challenge this interpretation? What alternative forms of prayer are emerging, and what further strategies are needed?

In order to respond to these questions, I will bring together the earliest strata of how Christians have prayed in the name of Jesus with ways in which contemporary churches, in their published liturgies, appropriate that tradition or transform it. The next step will be to consider some of the contemporary feminist approaches to the identity and meaning of Jesus and contemporary feminist strategies for bringing together feminist and Christian identity in prayer.

Prayer in the Name of Jesus

"So, could you not stay awake with me one hour? Stay awake and pray that you may not come into the time of trial; the spirit indeed is willing, but the flesh is weak."

Matthew 26:40b-41.

Earliest Christian prayer is not very different from Jewish prayer of the first century of the Common Era. Paul Bradshaw notes that during this period Jewish daily prayer was not yet firmly fixed, either in content or in form. Various forms were common, certain times of day were in general use, but the content of the prayers to be said daily was flexible. In the same way, daily (and weekly) Christian prayer reflects the use of forms in common with Jewish prayer, specifically the *berakah*, the *hodayah*, and the prayer of direct *anamnesis*, which were then filled with Christian content at regular times of the day and night. Thus the Lord's Prayer stands in continuity with this practice, with the variations in the texts recorded in the Gospels indicating its fluid oral character. The *Didache* instructs Christians to pray this prayer three times a day, but Bradshaw argues that it would not have been prayed alone, but placed within "normal Jewish forms" of daily prayer.[2]

Likewise, first-century Christian prayer reflects contemporary Jewish practice in its content. Petition and intercession figure prominently in a context of praise and proclamation; that is, Christian prayer of this period makes use of the *berakah/hodayah* form, which ascribes honor to God for past or present deeds and petitions God's further good will in light of those deeds.[3] God is addressed in titles of patriarchal honor and power: Father, Lord, Master, and Almighty.[4] Again, the use of these titles does not distinguish Christian prayer from Jewish prayer of the same period.

"The most distinctive feature" of Christian prayer, Bradshaw observes, is that it is offered "in the name of Jesus."[5] Bradshaw describes this practice as follows:

> ... some reference to Jesus would be included either in the opening address or in the anamnesis section of the prayer, as constituting the ground upon which petition might now be made, or in both, and it would be this which would fundamentally distinguish Christian prayer from that of other Jews.[6]

He also argues that this prayer practice may have been the original context of "confessing Jesus as Lord," rather than credal forms.

Also in continuity with Jewish prayer of the period is the Christian emphasis on eschatology. Like Jewish prayer, Christian prayers focus on waiting and expectation; prayer is offered facing east, the direction from which the Messiah is to come/return. Prayer at regular times of the day and especially during the night is a sign of readiness for the eschatological event. Indeed, as Bradshaw notes, "Prayer is regarded as the proper mode of eschatological vigilance."[7]

But what is the content of these vigilant prayers? Although Bradshaw argues that the thanksgiving-petition model is the prototypical Christian and Jewish prayer of the period, the Gospel texts that refer to eschatological vigilance suggest a slightly different focus. While some of the parables of the eschatological *basileia* depict it in celebratory images—a great feast, or a wedding feast—other parables and sayings suggest a more threatening context. For example, Luke 18:1-8 records the parable of the widow and the unjust judge, in which the widow's relentless demand for justice against her enemy eventually gets an answer. Traditional polite prayers of petition don't seem adequate to these purposes. The widow demands, she does not request. Moreover, the eschatological disasters described in the "little apocalypse" of Luke conclude with prayer advice:

> Be alert at all times, praying that you may have the strength to escape all these these things that will take place, and to stand before the Son of Man. (Luke 21:36)

This suggests not only demand for justice as part of eschatological praying, but also cries for deliverance from suffering. That prayers for escape from suffering and disaster are central to this earliest Christian practice is reflected in two other places in the Gospel as well. The Lord's Prayer includes a similar petition: "do not bring us to the time of trial, but rescue us from the evil one" (Matthew 6:13). And Jesus echoes this petition in the prayer in the Garden, where he is described as "grieved and agitated": "My Father, if it is possible, let this cup pass from me; yet not what I want, but what you want" (Matthew 26:39). Bradshaw draws attention to the three times that Jesus utters this prayer (verse 44:

"So leaving them again, he went away and prayed for the third time, saying the same words.") as a prototype of Christian prayer three times a day.[8] Thus we may conclude that first-century Christian prayer, like Jewish prayer of the same period, was fluid and flexible in formulation, was expected to be offered throughout the day and night, and carried the predominant note of eschatological expectation, which in turn mingled hope and anxiety. In particular, expectation or experience of disasters, both natural and political, give the prayers an emphasis on entreaties for rescue and demands for justice and relief. Christian prayers, prayed with reference to Jesus, focus not on his triumph or imperial reign, but on his own prayer for deliverance.

By contrast, later Christianity gradually assumed the patriarchal household model of the Greco-Roman culture, then the imperial model. Accordingly, Jesus came to be seen as the male head of the household or the cosmic emperor. As Elizabeth Johnson notes,

> Christ was then viewed as the principle of headship and cosmic order, the ruling king of glory, the Pantocrator par excellence, whose heavenly reign sets up and sustains the earthly rule of the head of the family, empire, and church.[9]

A brief survey of contemporary mainline liturgical books reveals that Jesus is overwhelmingly depicted in these regal, patriarchal images.[10] The most common forms of reference are Son, Lord, Savior, and Christ. Other ascriptions include: Master, Prince of Peace, Lord of this world, Lord of all, merciful and righteous Judge, Lord of love, the crucified one who now rules the world, our eternal brother, risen Christ, cornerstone, our hope and our true joy, our Redeemer, Sovereign and Savior, and our head, the Savior of the world. Clearly the elision of Jesus' authority and the authority of the emperor that occurred during the Christological controversies predominates here rather than the more ancient Jewish eschatological prayer practice that responds to injustice and suffering with resistance. Moreover, although intercession on behalf of the suffering of the world is found in all contemporary liturgical books, such intercessions do not reflect Jesus' advice to pray for avoidance of suffering or demands for justice.

Christian Feminist Reinterpretations of Jesus

Martha said to Jesus, "Lord, if you had been here, my brother would not have died."

John 11:21

Like Martha and Mary, Christian feminists know Jesus not only as the omnipresent and all-powerful savior and ruler of all, but also as the absent one. Christian feminist reinterpretation of Jesus, as with God, is generated out of this experience of absence, of lack of response to women's sufferings. The traditional Jesus, reflected in prayer and preaching, appears as divine, perfect, triumphant, and sovereign, as well as meek, self-sacrificial, and obedient to God his Father. And above all, Jesus is presented as male. Jesus' maleness, Jesus' obedient sonship, and Jesus' divine kingship create problems for Christian feminist prayer.

The maleness of Jesus forms the basis of contemporary Roman Catholic arguments against the ordination of women to the priesthood, a relatively new argument in the history of Christian restrictions against women's exercise of liturgical agency.[11] This emphasis on Jesus' maleness is presented in the context of patriarchal discourses that, as Elisabeth Schüssler Fiorenza notes,

> assume essential gender difference as a "common sense" biological given, [and thus] patriarchal theology can advance the maleness of Jesus as divinely revealed and historically given.[12]

This argument of divine revelation is related to language about God the Father, who is assumed to be revealed most perfectly in Jesus. Arguments about Jesus' historical maleness proceed on the basis of historical positivism and, in Schüssler Fiorenza's terms, "have endowed the biological sex of the historical Jesus with theological significance."[13]

Christian feminist theologians deal with the maleness of Jesus in several ways. Some of the earliest responses to the problem of the contemporary emphasis on the maleness of Jesus accept the importance of maleness, but relocate Jesus' uniqueness in his "feminist" or "feminine" character or behavior.[14] Others attempt to shift the theological emphasis away from Jesus' maleness to his humanity, thus moving from a dominant-male paradigm to a communal-relational paradigm. For example, Rosemary Radford Ruether reframes the figure of Jesus as "the representative of

94

liberated humanity and the liberating Word of God."[15] This representative function lies not in Jesus' suffering and death, as in traditional patriarchal theologies, but in "his person as a lived message and practice. . . . [of] good news to the poor, a confrontation with systems of religion and society that incarnate oppressive privilege, and an affirmation of the despised as loved and liberated by God."[16]

In a similar vein, Jacquelyn Grant argues that even though traditional male theology and white feminist theology have kept Jesus captive to systems of racial, gender, and class oppression, African American women have found meaning in Jesus' life and message that transcends such captivity. For them Jesus is "co-sufferer, equalizer, freedom, and liberator."[17] African theologians Mercy Amba Oduyoye and Elizabeth Amoah present African Christian women's Jesus as liberator, comrade, wise and powerful friend, giver of gifts.[18]

There are great strengths to these approaches. They all tend to decenter the meaning of Jesus away from his suffering and death and relocate it in his life and teaching. They all emphasize the political meaning of that life and teaching both in its historical context and in contemporary life. By emphasizing Jesus as liberator, this approach broadens the issue beyond the interests of middle-class North American white women to include all who suffer poverty, racism, classism, or sexism. Because of this broader commitment, this reading is more likely to recognize the political meaning of the life of Jesus. For example, Oduyoye and Amoah say that "the Christ of the theology of the people is the Christ who breaks the power of evil and empowers our life's journey."[19]

However, this approach to Jesus as liberator and representative of the New Humanity has been criticized as remaining too much within the patriarchal construct of humanity, which is always defined as normatively male, and for depending too heavily on the historical Jesus, with implications of historical positivism. Alternative proposals deconstruct the heroic liberator figure of Jesus and relocate redemptive meaning in the community. In the work of Elisabeth Moltmann-Wendell, Jesus is known and proclaimed primarily, and originally, through women.[20] However, Moltmann-Wendell still presents Jesus as the liberated or "feminized" man: "a Jesus . . . who challenges the male and human image still based on the constant independence, strength, and repression of feelings."[21] More radically, Rita Nakashima Brock rejects individualistic and heroic (even heroic male feminist) models of Jesus in order to place Jesus not at the center of the community but as a part of it, himself redeemed and healed by that community:

> Jesus participates centrally in this Christa/Community, but he neither brings erotic power into being nor controls it. He is brought into being through it and participates in the co-creation of it.[22]

This emphasis on the community as central and relationship as primary appears also in the work of Carter Heyward. Writing from the perspective of a lesbian feminist Christian, Heyward also rejects the traditional image of Jesus as heroic individual and emphasizes the primacy of relationships. She re-images Jesus as "Christa," communally and personally defined: "... in our shared commitment to human well-being, we are she: bearer and borne, mother and child. We are Christa."[23] Jesus is with us, and we are with Jesus; but Christ/Christa is in us. The value of these relational interpretations lies in their relocation of power and meaning away from the patriarchal pyramid of dominant-submissive power in community and relationship. However, the risk with all relational Christologies is that they can easily rewrite patriarchal definitions of "masculine" and "feminine" and thus ultimately fail to challenge patriarchal power. Women are culturally assigned the task of caring for relationships. Therefore, relational Christologies that emphasize Jesus as relational, or that locate feminist Christology in relationships, are unable to disrupt this conventional and dichotomous social structure.

Another important strain in feminist Christological thought emphasizes Jesus neither as heroic liberator nor as feminized community but Jesus as female. Some who take this approach draw on medieval mystics' language about Jesus as mother, although Caroline Walker Bynum has demonstrated that much of the tradition of Jesus as mother originated in male monastic communities and served the religious needs of celibate men rather than women.[24] However, this language has been developed in an original direction by Eleanor McLaughlin, who reads in the fluidity of gender symbolism of these mystics—who speak of "Mother Jesus, he"—a fluidity of gender identity she identifies with transvestism.[25] With this move McLaughlin attempts to avoid the patriarchal constructions of male and female identity as well as the limitations of historical positivism:

> . . . Jesus who was and is both "historical fact" and symbol, a man, is like a "cross-dresser," one who is not "caught" by the categories. . . . Christians believe in a Jesus "dressed" in the flesh, that most female of symbols, and they believe in a God in man-flesh who behaves like a woman. This "transvestite" Jesus makes a human space where no one is out of place because the notion of place and gender has been transformed.[26]

However, McLaughlin does not acknowledge the problem of dominance while attending to gender difference. "Flesh" is still identified with femaleness, recalling the Chalcedonian formula, where maleness is divine and femaleness is physical. Moreover, male transvestism is incorporated into patriarchal culture as entertainment whereas female transvestism has as its patron Joan of Arc, who was executed for assuming male dress. Jesus remains "historically male" but in female "dress," which in and of itself does not disrupt the dominant discourse that finds males dressed as women amusing.

Another attempt to construct a female Jesus is based on the recovery of the biblical image of Sophia, or Wisdom, a model that has been particularly influential in the development of feminist prayer and ritual. Feminist scholars who have most thoroughly developed this approach are Elisabeth Schüssler Fiorenza and Elizabeth Johnson. Schüssler Fiorenza's research has approached the subject as a New Testament scholar, while Johnson is a systematic theologian. Thus they bring differing methods and questions to the issue. Since our questions have to do primarily with prayer rather than systematic or biblical questions, we will briefly examine both scholars' conclusions before turning to issues of prayer in the name of Jesus.

Johnson's work applies Sophia imagery to Jesus by distinguishing between the human male Jesus on the one hand and the communal Christ on the other:

> The fundamental nature of Christian identity as life in Christ makes clear that the biblical symbol Christ, the one anointed in the Spirit, cannot be restricted to the historical person Jesus nor to certain select members of the community but signifies all those who by drinking of the Spirit participate in the community of disciples.[27]

Having made this distinction, Johnson is simultaneously able to safeguard the maleness of Jesus as "a constitutive element of his identity, part of the perfection and limitation of his historical contingency," and to present Jesus the male as "wisdom's child, Sophia incarnate," who is able to invoke "Sophia's characteristic gracious goodness, life-giving creativity and passion for justice."[28] Johnson names this identification of Jesus with Sophia as a "paradox . . . [that] points the way to a reconciliation of opposites and their transformation from enemies into a liberating, unified diversity."[29] In addition, she argues that such language bears additional benefits in reclaiming a connection to the cosmos and thus to ecological concerns, in emphasizing global human inclusivity, and in privileging justice-seeking as the work of the community identified with Sophia-Jesus.[30] However, the association of Sophia with patriarchally-defined female tasks such as care for environment and for inclusive human relationships and with "feminine" values such as "gracious goodness and life-giving creativity" point to the patriarchal context of the biblical Sophia literature. Without critical assessment of that context, feminist appropriation of Wisdom tradition runs the risk of reinscribing patriarchal "feminine" models on divine images, whether of Jesus or of God. As long as patriarchal "opposites" are only "reconciled" and not disrupted and eliminated, the patriarchal pattern of gender dominance remains unchallenged.

Some feminist scholars have drawn attention to the patriarchal context of Wisdom literature and argued that it is thus unhelpful for feminist use. Luise Schottroff in particular has pointed to the origin of Wisdom literature in the teaching of elite males, and argues that the feminist appropriation of this tradition runs the risk of obscuring the Gospel's more radical identification with the poor, the majority of whom are women and children dependent on women.[31]

Schüssler Fiorenza agrees with Schottroff's assessment of the elite context of most Wisdom literature, but not with her absolute rejection of it as a feminist resource. Schüssler Fiorenza finds the "early 'Jesus messenger of Sophia' traditions" useful for feminist Christology because they locate Jesus firmly in a Jewish milieu that integrates and democratizes the Wisdom tradition within the proclamation of the egalitarian *basileia* and without resorting to anti-Jewish arguments of superiority and exclusivism.[32]

However, unlike other feminist scholars who wish to employ Sophia imagery for feminist Christology, Schüssler Fiorenza insists that this tradition cannot be recovered "to become the essential feminist tradition of Christianity," nor does its reconstruction "necessarily provide a tradition usable for feminists and liberationists."[33] Instead she wants to propose that feminist Christology must proceed from a critical perspective on the sociocultural character of language. Feminist Christological discourse must resist linguistic determinism that assumes that language is an accurate reflection of reality, but also it must resist "playfully relativistic" postmodernist approaches. Instead, Schüssler Fiorenza argues,

> Feminist theology must rearticulate the symbols, images, and names of Divine Sophia in the context of our own experiences and theological struggles in such a way that the ossified and absolutized masculine language about G*d and Christ is radically questioned and undermined and the Western cultural sex/gender system is radically deconstructed.[34]

But how is this rearticulation to be done? What are the shapes that it might take, and how best to proceed in the process of undermining and dismantling the oppressive systems in which the church and theology operate? Schüssler Fiorenza does not specify, but refers readers to liturgical and spiritual exercises. A significant (but not sole) site for this process is in the experience of prayer and ritual.

Finally, an approach found primarily among women of the Third World, less tied to Western Christian dogmatic theologies and historical worldviews, employ a rich variety of images for Jesus that are male, female, human, and nonhuman. For example, Oduyoye and Amoah cite Ghanian theologian Afua Kuma. For Afua, "Yesu" is rock for hiding, a bush which creates cooling shade, a giant tree that provides a view of heaven to the climber, and "the Pensil," the means of transmitting knowledge to children by teachers.[35] Also from an African adaptation of the story of Jesus comes the idea of Jesus as deliverer. As Oduyoye and Amoah remark, in African cultures "deliverers abound; some are memorialized in legends, but they are not always male." The African context creates the possibility of many Christs, "persons in whom the Spirit of God dwells in all its fullness," both in the past and into the future.[36] These strategies provide models of alternative interpretations of Jesus that displace Western concern with doctrine and history, and create a poetic, creative cultural context for reinterpretation.

How, in light of the issues identified by these and other feminist theologians, are we to pray "in the name of Jesus"? What strategies and reconstructions must be created? These questions cannot be answered before a consideration of the second feminist problem with Jesus in liturgical prayer: the meaning of his suffering and death.

The Suffering of Jesus and the Suffering of Women

> At three o'clock Jesus cried out with a loud voice, "Eloi, Eloi, lema sabachthani?" which means, "My God, my God, why have you forsaken me?"
>
> Mark 15:34

The suffering and death of Jesus stands at the center of Christian theology, identity, and liturgy. The struggle to understand and interpret the event of Jesus' death occupies the writers of the New Testament as well as Christian theologians of every age and place, and permeates the history of Christian worship and prayer.

This is not the place to attempt even a review, let alone a reconstruction, of Christian doctrines of the atonement and the symbolism of the cross. However, certain aspects of this doctrine must be considered as part of the process of coming to an understanding of what it means for feminists to pray "in the name of Jesus."

Liberationist and feminist theologians have identified the traditional means of working out this meaning of Jesus' death as a central issue; however, they have approached the problem of the suffering and death of Jesus differently. Where liberation theologians have seen in the suffering of Jesus a sign that God is with the poor and the victimized in their pain, that God indeed suffers with them, feminist theologians have pointed to the harm done, particularly to women, by connecting suffering with love and redemption. In what is perhaps the most succinct and pointed critique of this problem, Joanne Carlson Brown and Rebecca Parker review traditional and contemporary doctrines of the atonement and conclude that "Christianity is an abusive theology that glorifies suffering."[37]

In response to this critique, some feminist theologians have attempted to reconstruct not only the Christ symbol but also the symbol of the cross. Mary Grey, for example, argues from a symbolic standpoint, interpreting traditional readings of the cross as inadequate, but resymbolizing the cross as a sign of "at-one-ment" and "birth."[38] In a similar vein, Elizabeth Johnson argues that

> Guided by wisdom categories, the story of the cross, rejected as passive, penal victimization, is reappropriated as heartbreaking empowerment. The suffering accompanying such a life as Jesus led is neither passive, useless, nor divinely ordained, but is linked to the ways of Sophia forging justice and peace in an antagonistic world. As such, the cross is part of the larger mystery of pain-to-life, of that struggle for the new creation evocative of the rhythm of pregnancy, delivery, and birth so familiar to women of all times.[39]

But the cross is not a story about pain but about death. Such attempts to redeem death by aligning it with birth fail to recognize that birth is not about bringing life from death, but about bringing life from life. Moreover, to argue that the pain of childbirth is somehow intrinsic to the process reiterates male medical and theological arguments that women should not receive pain-killing medicine during childbirth because their pain was divinely ordained by God as part of punishment for the fall (Genesis 3:16).

The argument that Jesus' suffering and death is a consequence of his radical life is not unique to feminist theologians. It is a particularly strong theme in liberation theologies and in theologies based on principles of nonviolent resistance. Such theologies not only see suffering as purposeful when freely chosen as a means to inspire others or to act with integrity, but also see the suffering of Jesus on the cross as a sign of God's solidarity with those who suffer. This identification of the suffering of Jesus with the suffering of the poor or oppressed is also a cornerstone of much Asian feminist theology. Korean feminist theologian Chung Hyun Kyung identifies the Jesus of Asian women as the Suffering Servant, and Hong Kong theologian Kwok Pui-Lan argues that Jesus is "the God who takes the human form and suffers and weeps with us."[40]

101

However, the risks of this argument are great. The view that Jesus' suffering is a consequence of a life of integrity and radical liberation reinforces assumptions about the value of martyrdom. The martyr as inspiration and heroic model is common to most cultures, but it is a model that glorifies suffering and limits outrage and resistance. Willingness to be martyred supports violent and abusive use of power. Seeing Jesus as a martyr, a willing victim, also ignores his prayer for deliverance in the Garden of Gethsemane as well as his advice to others to avoid martyrdom.

A further problem with the argument as constructed by Grey and Johnson lies in their use of pregnancy and birth symbolism to speak of the cross. Schüssler Fiorenza notes that this symbolic approach is misplaced, and that the reimaging in positive terms should focus rather on the resurrection, since this reimaging of the cross "cannot but depoliticize and spiritualize Jesus' execution in 'feminine' terms."[41] By adopting birth imagery to refer to a brutal political execution, this argument also renders pregnancy and childbirth in terms of sacrifice, suffering, and death, as well as universalizing an experience that is not shared by all women.

What is often lost sight of, already in the New Testament and in subsequent Christian reflection on the crucifixion of Jesus, is that the death of Jesus was a brutal political execution that was not unique in the ancient world (it was a common Roman method of disposing of political prisoners) but that was evidently not expected by his companions. As Schüssler Fiorenza points out, the writers of the Christian scriptures reflect a variety of rhetorical strategies that attempt to make sense of this terrible event. One of the strategies that was generally not available to them, it might be added, is open outrage. As Schüssler Fiorenza notes,

> . . . the execution of Jesus . . . created the need for a political apologetics capable of showing that the early Christians were not seditious enemies of the Roman order. Such a political apologetics had to shift theological attention away from the political character of the death of Jesus to a religious symbolic interpretation of the cross and away from the culpability of the Roman imperial administration to that of the Jewish leadership and people.[42]

It is precisely these moves, from political meaning to religious, and from openly named culpability to scapegoating, that make it so difficult for Christians to confront suffering and oppression directly. Carlson Brown and Parker have argued forcefully that "Christianity has been a primary—in many women's lives *the* primary—force in shaping our acceptance of abuse."[43] They locate the problem primarily in women's acceptance of our own abuse. But it is not only women, of course, who accept our abuse. Even when we resist (an action for which there are few models in traditional Christian theology), the religious world in which we live will attempt to spiritualize our suffering and prevent us from naming the offenders. North American feminist theologian Millicent C. Feske raises the same issue from the perspective of materialist feminist thought, drawing attention to the inability of contemporary women's narratives to envision "a future characterized by women's desires for freedom, joy, pleasure, and wholeness," that instead offer "characters who seemingly must and do die, and whose deaths are presented to us as acceptable endings to their narratives."[44] Feske demonstrates that prominent contemporary narratives of women suggest that "the only apparent choice for women who embody resistance and seek a fuller existence is death."[45] Christian theologies of redemption as suffering and death contribute to this problem, she argues.

What resources are there for resisting and naming the violence and abuse? What strategies of prayer can disrupt the discourse of spiritualization and scapegoating of suffering offered "in the name of Jesus"? And what strategies are necessary for women and other oppressed people to be able to envision a world in which women's hopes and desires for pleasure and freedom are realizable? Feske proposes that:

> it is essential that women be able to imagine their redemption in both fiction and theology in ways that will bear fruit concretely in terms of the ability to resist restrictive or abusive social relationships without fear of retribution and to experience lives constituted by women's hopes and desires for wholeness and healing.[46]

As Carlson Brown and Parker put it, it is necessary to envision redemption in terms of resistance rather than suffering: "Resurrection means that death is overcome in those precise instances when human beings choose life, refusing the threat of death."[47] Delores Williams comes to a similar conclusion when she rejects the surrogate role of Jesus in doctrines of the atonement as inappropriate for black women who have historically been exploited as surrogates. Williams wishes to "free redemption from the cross and free the cross from the 'sacred aura' put around it by existing patriarchal responses to the question of what Jesus' death represents."[48] In its place she would identify redemption with life, rather than death: "The spirit of God came in Jesus to show humans *life*. . . ."[49] Oduyoye and Amoah identify resistance to suffering with the meaning of Jesus in Africa:

> In Africa, where suffering seems endemic, where hunger and thirst are the continuous experience of millions, a suffering Christ becomes an attractive figure. However, Jesus of Nazareth is seen more as a comrade who did not accept deprivation as the destiny of humanity, but rather, demonstrated in his dealings with people that such suffering is not in the plan of God.[50]

Filipino theologian Virginia Fabella points out that "numerous Filipino women are undergoing this apparently passive moment of Jesus' suffering," but also that the passion of Jesus, reinterpreted as an act of solidarity and resistance, "is relived among the militant, protesting Filipino women who have taken up the struggle on behalf of their sisters and the rest of the suffering poor."[51]

Korean women, interpreting the suffering of women with the Korean concept of *han*, or unjustified suffering, understand redemption as being exorcised from their burden of *han*: "If Jesus Christ is to make sense to us, then Jesus Christ must be an exorcist of our *han*."[52] Thus Jesus' suffering and death is placed in the context of the ongoing suffering of women, particularly Third World women, rather than being interpreted as a special, unique, or glorified form of suffering.

Finally, the experience of battered and abused women brings a necessary perspective to a feminist theology of suffering. As Carol J. Adams observes, "Numerous battered women report that their clergy encouraged them to return to their abuser and offered the model of Christ's suffering."[53] To counter this use of the suffering of Jesus to justify the suffering of women, Adams contrasts the suffering of Jesus with the suffering of the battered woman:

> Jesus' experience of suffering was finite; if nothing changes her suffering is potentially infinite. . . . Jesus was only crucified once. And while that was a painful, tragic, awful day, Jesus never had to face that day again. What about her situation? Sometimes beatings

and the accompanying abusive treatment may last for hours. . . .
How many Good Fridays must she endure before she, like Jesus,
never has to face those days again?[54]

By distinguishing the suffering inflicted on women by battering
partners from the suffering of Jesus, Adams disrupts the conventional interpretations in a way that calls for an end to suffering.
However, as Adams notes, Jesus' death is not the final theological
word, but his resurrection is. She urges battered women to claim
the resurrection as a resource for their own *no* to the violence.

To summarize, Christian feminist theologians reject traditional interpretations of Jesus' suffering and death that assume
his political innocence, his obedience, his unquestioning acceptance, his martyrdom, his surrogate or sacrificial role. In the
words of Carlson Brown and Parker, "suffering is never redemptive and suffering cannot be redeemed."[55] Instead, Jesus' death is
reinterpreted as a violent and brutal political execution, not unlike the violent and brutal political murders that go on around
the world today and every day. If we want to avoid glorifying and
mystifying these contemporary deaths, we cannot glorify or mys-
tify the death of Jesus either. In a post-Holocaust age, more
martyrs are not needed. Survival, not death, is glorious. And the
resurrection of Jesus then must be read not as a reward to Jesus
for having endured the cross, but as a sign of God's resistance to
and refusal of death, God's *no* to suffering and death, and *yes* to
life.

Traditional Christian Prayer and the Suffering of Jesus

Almighty God, whose most dear Son went not up to joy but first
he suffered pain, and entered not into glory before he was crucified:
Mercifully grant that we, walking in the way of the cross, may find
it none other than the way of life and peace.

Collect for Palm Sunday, *Book of Common Prayer*, 1979.

Traditional Christian prayer focuses most directly on the suffering and death of Jesus in the liturgies of Holy Week and Easter.
Beginning with Palm/Passion Sunday, the church enters into a
dramatic ritual interpretation of the final days of Jesus' life. Contemporary worship resources unite in emphasizing the restoration of the ancient church's pattern for observing these events in

the *Triduum Sacrum*, the Three Holy Days of Holy (or Maundy) Thursday, Good Friday, and the Great Vigil on Holy Saturday. Following the restoration of this three-day cycle of liturgy by the Roman Catholic Church as part of the reforms of Vatican II, mainline Protestant churches in North America have introduced this cycle, or some variation of it, into their revised liturgical books.

These revisions emphasize the centrality of these observances of the suffering and death of Jesus as being both necessary to an adequate understanding of the resurrection and as the most focused observance of the central meaning of Christian faith. The authors of *The New Handbook of the Christian Year*, a United Methodist resource, explain:

> The aim of these three great days of observance is to proclaim the events of our Lord's passion and death, and to awaken in us a sense of God's ever-present saving power through the cross and resurrection. . . . By faithful participation in the liturgy of Holy Week and Easter, we encounter Christ who, through his redemptive suffering and death and his triumphant rising, comes to deliver all humanity from bondage and death.[56]

Clearly the purpose of these services, then, is not mere historical representation, but congregational participation. Participants are to interpret Jesus' suffering and death as redemptive and necessary. The Presbyterian commentary on the liturgical year relates this interconnection between suffering and resurrection with congregational spirituality:

> Because of this interrelationship of the three days, each service of the Triduum needs the others to tell the whole story. For example, resurrection is incomprehensible without Christ's self-giving in crucifixion and at the Lord's Supper. Therefore, Easter needs Good Friday and Maundy Thursday to be fully understood. The way to the triumph of Easter is through the Triduum.
>
> All of Holy Week, and particularly its three concluding days (the Triduum), provides an opportunity to undertake a pilgrimage of renewed commitment and joy: to travel Christ's path of servanthood through the Lord's Supper and the suffering of the cross, as we move toward Easter.[57]

What story is told in these liturgies? As these commentaries suggest, the suffering and death of Jesus is interpreted as redemptive in itself and as leading to the triumph of the resurrection. The model of Jesus as heroic victor is very strong here. The victorious interpretation of the resurrection is anticipated in the liturgy for Palm/Passion Sunday (also called, variously, "Passion/Palm Sunday," "The Sunday of the Passion: Palm Sunday,") with its emphasis on the "triumphal entry" of Jesus into Jerusalem, and with the opening collect that includes the phrase, "Let these branches be for us signs of his victory. . . ."[58] The intimate connection between victory and suffering is already implied by combining in this one liturgy the triumphal entry and the narration of the Passion of Jesus by means of a dramatic reading of one of the synoptic accounts. The connection is made clear in the prayer for blessing the palms in the United Church of Christ *Book of Worship*:

> . . . In these events of defeat and victory,
> you have sealed the closeness
> of death and resurrection,
> of humiliation and exaltation.
> We thank you for these branches
> that promise to become for us
> symbols of martyrdom and majesty. . . .[59]

Although the commentaries sometimes refer to this "closeness of humiliation and exaltation" as irony or paradox, all the services of this passion season emphasize this connection. The humility of Jesus is stressed in Holy Thursday/Maundy Thursday services that include the ritual of foot-washing: "My sisters and brothers, Christ shows his love by becoming a humble servant."[60] The innocent and redemptive suffering of Jesus is strongest in the Good Friday liturgies, that can include readings from the Suffering Servant songs of Isaiah 52–53 with their emphasis not only on substitutionary suffering, but also silent submission to suffering; Psalm 22; and John's passion narrative. Similarly, as the redemption and victory of the resurrection is read through the lens of suffering and death in Palm Sunday, Holy Thursday, and Good Friday liturgies, the close connection also appears in the Easter liturgy, especially the Great Vigil. The Exsultet, the ancient hymn to the Paschal candle, refers to the triumph of Christ over death in terms both of Passover and of ransom:

> For Christ has ransomed us with his blood,
> and paid the debt of Adam's sin to deliver your
> faithful people.

This is our Passover feast, when Christ, the true Lamb, is
slain.[61]

Images of Jesus as silent and submissive, of his death as sacrifice,
as payment of debt, as substitutionary or vicarious suffering,
abound in these liturgies. Jesus' resurrection is tied closely with
his salvific suffering and death, being seen not only as a victory
over death, but as necessarily requiring passing through suffering
and death. Jesus as the one who resists his own suffering and
death, as one who teaches his companions not to seek or accept
it, but to pray to avoid it, is not present. The struggle of Jesus in
the Garden, and his own prayer to be relieved of his suffering and
death, is read only on Palm/Passion Sunday when the "long
reading" is used. It is not part of the Good Friday liturgy.

Christian Feminist Prayer and Jesus

O God whose word is life,
and whose delight is to answer our cry,
give us faith like the Syro-Phoenician woman,
who refused to remain an outsider:
that we too may have the wit to argue
and demand that our daughters be made whole,
through Jesus Christ, Amen.

Janet Morley, *All Desires Known*[62]

Christian feminist prayer employs a rich variety of strategies
regarding the symbolism of Jesus. Prayer and ritual are central
places where the symbolizing of a world in which God desires
and Jesus embraces the joy, hope, and well-being of women takes
place. How do feminists in prayer set about creating this symbolizing space?

Christian feminists are, at best, ambivalent about the role of
Jesus in traditional theology and prayer. As Miriam Therese Winter, Adair Lummis, and Alison Stokes, the authors of a major
survey of North American Christian women's religious lives,
note,

In 'women-church' groups where most of the meeting time is spent
in ritual and the image of God is pivotal to the group, more often
than not Jesus is simply ignored.[63]

The pain and ambivalence that fuels this marginalization of the role of Jesus is eloquently expressed by a United Church of Christ clergywoman who participated in the study:

> I am a Christian whose images of God have not been Christ-centered and for whom the image of Christ as sacrifice is very destructive. How do other women experience God? Am I the only one who has trouble with Christ? As someone ordained who has functionally been out of the church institution for several years, I have so many feelings I have not worked out yet. There is a lot of pain there.[64]

A survey of published contemporary feminist prayers intended for corporate use reveals several strategies at work, often within the same liturgy or ritual. A widely used strategy reflects this pain and rejection by omitting references to Jesus in prayer or ritual. For example, *Birthings and Blessings*, a collection of liturgies clearly tied to the Christian year calendar (a Christological cycle) for use by a women's group in a North American Presbyterian church, includes a service for Advent and one for Lent that make no reference to Jesus, even though the editors' commentaries on the services make it perfectly clear that the liturgies are Christian.[65] The Advent liturgy draws on the work of the late North American feminist theologian Nelle Morton and the title of the service is taken from her final work: "The Journey Is Home." It uses the image of the journey as a symbol of Advent, thus moving what is traditionally a season emphasizing waiting (a passive model) into a season of journeying, of movement. The Lenten service is a penitential service that reframes the idea of penitence and sin in feminist terms. Jesus thus is not addressed directly in this strategy, but only obliquely, by means of context or season. Jesus' absence, as in Martha's accusation in the death of her brother, becomes the means of Jesus' representation. In the same way, North American Catholic Diann Neu describes the design of a feminist celebration of Pentecost that focuses not on the resurrected Jesus or the male disciples but on women:

> "Women of Fire" reclaims for women the traditional Christian feast of Pentecost. This major feast celebrates the birth of the Christian church and the renewal of ministry and community in the Holy Spirit. "Women of Fire" focuses on the power of the Spirit within her people, including women's full participation in ministry and community and church for the transformation of injustice. The

109

feminist liturgical text . . . celebrates the power of the Spirit received by women. It celebrates women's passion, pain, politics, and promise in a liturgy that includes Eucharist. It reclaims Pentecost as a time when women-church came to life.[66]

By employing traditional Christian seasons as a framework for feminist ritualizing and prayer, and by shifting the focus away from Jesus, these liturgies reframe the meaning of Jesus and of Christian identity in terms of contemporary (not biblical) women.

A second strategy is the use of symbolic referent. For example, an Advent liturgy in *Birthings and Blessings* uses "a large Christ candle" as the visual centerpiece of a liturgy called "The Holy Emerges from the Darkness." Since no further description of this candle is provided, the writers clearly assume (and correctly, no doubt) that readers will know that a large white pillar candle is meant. Since the readings, prayers and meditation focus on the annunciation to Mary, Jesus is present only in this lighted candle and as promise. Similarly, in Advent prayers in several feminist publications, the focus is on Mary, with Jesus represented as an infant or child.

A third strategy is to focus on or address Jesus more directly, but in the context of his relationships with biblical women. The prayer quoted above, by British feminist Janet Morley, concludes with a traditional invocation of the name of Jesus, but the basis for the petition is not Jesus but the Syro-Phoenician woman who demands that Jesus heal her daughter. This resists the practice of traditional prayers that use Jesus' behavior as a basis for petitions.

A fourth strategy employs Sophia imagery to refer to Jesus, either somewhat obliquely or directly. Out of awareness of the biblical research on the theological image of Sophia and its application in Christian writings to Jesus, this strategy has become very popular in feminist prayer. The most thoroughgoing example of this strategy is found in *Wisdom's Feast: Sophia in Study and Celebration*, by Susan Cady, Hal Taussig, and Marian Ronan. They developed an extended series of liturgies, prayers, and rituals based on the biblical image of Sophia for use in study groups, women's groups, and congregations. Some of their material substitutes the name Sophia in the place of Jesus in traditional hymns and liturgical texts.[67] It does this most dramatically in the "Sophia Passion in Three Parts" designed for use by a women's group that had been studying Sophia. In these three interconnecting liturgies, Jesus is represented as Sophia, as a "response to the needs of the contemporary community."[68] Based on the chronology of John's gospel and following the liturgical tradition of the *Triduum Sacrum*, the Three Holy Days of the passion of Jesus, the three services were a footwashing, a reenactment of the trial and crucifixion, and a celebration of the resurrection, focusing on the appearance of Jesus-Sophia to Mary Magdalene in the Garden. In each service, Sophia is substituted for Jesus in the Johannine account, and the symbolism is allowed to grow out of that beginning. The list of "charges" against Sophia, developed by the group in the Good Friday ritual, demonstrates well how a focus on Jesus-Sophia as a woman shifts the symbolic ground:

"You're just a woman."
"You're getting out of hand; you don't know your place."
"You participate in witchcraft and the work of the devil."
"You don't have any place in the church."
"You're not as strong and powerful as the male God."
"You are trying to usurp God's power."
"You are heresy."
"You're a slut."
"You're a cheap broad."
"You're a castrating bitch."
"You're not a real goddess; you're too minor; you're not important
    enough."
"Who do you think you are, acting like you're equal to God?"
"You're silly and foolish."
"You're evil; you're the gateway of the devil."
"God can't be a woman."[69]

It is instructive to note that in the liturgy it was understood that "Sophia stood on trial as the representative of all women who have been unjustly accused."[70] Prophetically, the accusations these participants have identified with Sophia have been leveled at them and other women participating in Christian liturgies invoking Sophia.[71] The liturgy concluded with a remembrance of women who had suffered and died, thus identifying them with Jesus-Sophia.

This approach to Jesus in feminist prayer is the most dramatic, the most prophetic, and the most threatening to patriarchal church power, as the accusations against Jesus-Sophia show. By remythologizing Jesus as Sophia these liturgies resist the temptations to feminize Jesus, thus reinscribing patriarchal definitions of sex and gender, or to cast Jesus as a "feminist," with the accompanying anti-Jewish bias. However, these liturgies also show the limitations of this approach if the biblical-liturgical tradition is accepted uncritically, since Jesus' resistance to his own suffering and death is obscured in the biblical texts used here and even more so in the liturgical tradition of the *Triduum Sacrum*. Therefore the sufferings and deaths of women commemorated in the Good Friday liturgy were recalled and honored in the Easter vigil liturgy, but there was no room for recognition of resistance either on the part of the women commemorated or on the part of the participants. Jesus-Sophia's solidarity with the suffering of women is made explicit; but the problem of the justification of suffering is not resolved.

Feminist strategies for praying "in the name of Jesus" thus range from the use of silence and absence, the use of nonverbal symbolic referent, the relational representation of Jesus in the company of women, to the elision of Jesus with the female image of Sophia. Each strategy has its integrity. Both the absence approach and the relational strategy move the attention away from its traditional location in Jesus as ruler and king or as model and exemplar to contemporary and biblical women. The "symbolic referent" strategy leaves the meaning of prayer "in the name of Jesus" open-ended, as symbols are. The Jesus-Sophia strategy confronts directly the mythologizing of Jesus in prayer and ritual and reconceives Jesus as a woman surrounded by friends and facing her suffering and death.

However, insofar as any of these strategies adopt uncritically the biblical accounts of Jesus or the liturgical interpretation of his life and death, they will finally be unable to resist the patriarchal ordering of sex and gender that includes acceptance and justification of women's suffering, and will not be able to make room for the struggle against suffering. Feminist prayer "in the name of Jesus" must resist patriarchal ordering, as Jesus did before his death, claim the resurrection as God's refusal of suffering, and at the same time expand the radical female mythologies of Jesus beyond the limitations of the biblical Sophia.

And what of nonhuman images of Jesus? Wisdom's Feast includes a Good Friday liturgy that reimages the story of Jesus' crucifixion as the cutting down of a tree. In contrast to the traditional crucifixion symbol of the cross as a "tree," here Jesus-Sophia is represented as a tree. Chung Hyun Kyung speaks of Jesus as grain, as food for hungry people.[72] Can such "natural" images function in an emancipatory way for feminist prayer? Pushing the Jesus image to include the nonhuman world is useful and meaningful as long as "Jesus" is understood as the primary or only manifestation of the divine in the world. However, this seems to assume a very "high" Christology. One need only to recall the traditional image of Jesus as Lamb to see that a nonresistant and exclusivist model of Jesus does not necessarily lead to emancipatory images when simply applied without critique to nonhuman beings. In the Good Friday liturgy of the tree, the tree does not resist its own destruction; in traditional Good Friday liturgies, the Lamb is a model of acquiesence to its own slaughter. Nonhuman beings are, in short, usually assumed to be passive and thus cannot themselves fund a resistant model, but must be reinterpreted, as is being done in animal rights theology.[73] Because of this passive image assigned to nonhuman beings in Western patriarchal thinking, and because nonhuman nature is imagined to exist for human use and exploitation, such imagery may also serve to spiritualize and minimize the reality of Jesus' suffering and thus of all suffering, human as well as nonhuman. In Janet Morley's words, for our own survival and well-being, we need "the wit to argue and demand" in our relationship with biblical and liturgical texts and traditions and with the patriarchal image of Jesus.

OUR BODIES, OUR BLOOD
Christian Feminist
Eucharistic Praying

How can we point to the eucharistic bread and say "This is my body" as long as women's bodies are battered, raped, sterilized, mutilated, prostituted, and used to male ends?

Elisabeth Schüssler Fiorenza, *In Memory of Her*[1]

For Christian feminists, the churches' eucharistic liturgy, commemorating the death and resurrection of Jesus in the context of a ritual meal, creates theological, spiritual, and political problems. It is commonplace to find among Christian feminists either lack of interest in or active rejection of the churches' traditional observance of this liturgy, variously called Holy Communion, the Eucharist, or the Lord's Supper.

The reasons for this are many. Some women, from churches that deny women access to liturgical presidency at the eucharistic table, find this absence of women the central problem, and the altar or communion table the symbol for this denial. For others, the altar-table symbolizes more generalized contempt for and exploitation of women. The use of exclusive language in prayer texts, the predominance of male presiders, the denial of women's voices in decision-making processes, all contribute to the sense of alienation many Christian women feel toward the church's worship. This alienation in some cases expresses itself in the form of absence from worship. A Roman Catholic woman comments,

I have gone from a very devout Catholic deeply involved in liturgy to someone who rarely even attends Mass. As my feminist consciousness has grown, I find myself feeling very uncomfortable in

115

a patriarchal church whose past and present continue to oppress women.[2]

This deep discomfort arises, at least in part, from a new consciousness of the church's participation in the exploitation of women. A woman who lost a job at her church makes the connection between her negative experience and participation in communion:

> Am I hurt and bitter? Yes. . . . I often wonder why people, especially women, remain Catholic when they are oppressed. For me, it gets hard to celebrate the Eucharist when I know the politics of the church.[3]

At times this strategy of women absenting themselves from the eucharistic liturgy arises not only from deep disillusionment but also from a desire to resist, to protest. As Winter, Lummis, and Stokes observe, for Roman Catholic women, "staying away goes straight to the heart of patriarchal issues, for the Catholic Church still treats weekly participation as a moral obligation, saying Catholics *must* go to Mass on Sunday."[4] This sense of obligation in combination with a deep love for the liturgy of the eucharist, creates considerable tension and pain for Catholic feminists. One of Winter, Lummis, and Stokes' informants, a Catholic woman from the West coast, expresses this tension dramatically:

> Though I love the Eucharist and believe in the church as community, I feel undervalued as a woman in the church. I often feel so angry that I imagine myself standing to scream out my frustration. I believe I will quit going before that happens.[5]

For Protestant women also, the service of Holy Communion, although not as central as in Roman Catholic liturgical life, still serves as a kind of ritual lightning rod for alienation and disillusionment with the institutional church. The male symbolism of God and Jesus, the dominance of male clergy as presiders, the presentation of Jesus as sacrifice and his death as necessary, the connection in Protestantism particularly between communion and forgiveness of sin, all create problems for feminist Christians.

For survivors of violence and for those working with them, all of these issues are intensified, where Jesus' triumphant suffering contrasts with the unrelieved suffering of the abused child or battered woman, where relationships of dominance and submission played out in the ritual at the table replicate abusive relationships, where rhetoric about innocent suffering and sacrifice and obedience to death spiritualize the remembered or ongoing suffering of the victims of male violence and abuse. The symbolism of bread and wine/body and blood as redemptive mystifies the real blood shed and real bodies broken in violence and abuse. Issues of body, of sin and forgiveness, of love and sacrifice, are raised in this ritual in ways that are rarely if ever nourishing to the survivor.[6]

Feminist dissatisfaction with the liturgy of the eucharist is located in this context of violence and abuse of women's bodies, a context that raises radical questions about the appropriateness of a ritually reiterated commemoration and—in some ways of thinking—re-presentation of an abused but glorified male body. This discomfort is also located in the context of associations of women with sin and unworthiness and reception of communion with worthiness. And it is also located in the context of traditional rejections of women's liturgical agency as presiders at the eucharistic ritual. Feminist critiques of the image of God, of the role of Jesus, of the value of sacrifice and obedience considered earlier in this study, come into sharp ritual focus in the liturgy of the eucharist. Text, action, gesture, leadership pattern, all must be reconsidered in light of these concerns.

The Anglican priest who prayed between the lines to read "This is my body," "This is my blood" as references to and celebration of her woman's body and blood is reading against the traditional interpretation of the text, and of the event. Not only does the traditional reading glorify a male body and sanctify bodily suffering, it also repels the inclusion of any female imagery.

Feminist critiques of Christian eucharistic practice usually proceed from three points. The first is the political, arguing that the denial of women's leadership at the altar renders the liturgy of the altar offensive and oppressive. This argument proceeds primarily from Roman Catholic and, until the ordination of Anglican women priests, Anglican feminists. A related argument insists that the denial of women's access to altar presidency is but a symptom of the churches' general disregard and denial of women's agency in multiple locations.

A second form of critique has focused on the use of exclusive male language in the prayers. The character of this critique and the possibilities for amelioration depend on the practice of the tradition. Some churches emphasize the canonical nature of official prayers, with the effect that the texts of the prayers are both more significant and more resistant to change. Other churches, in particular so-called free churches, may publish eucharistic texts, but those texts have no canonical status and thus may be changed by any presider. Still other churches publish no prayer texts as official texts, but presume a strong tradition of practice that would be recognized by worshipers, as would departures from the traditional practice. Some churches have published "inclusive language" eucharistic texts, primarily minimizing the use of male language and in some cases exploring the use of female God-language by drawing primarily on biblical images, particularly Wisdom-Sophia.

A third feminist critique addresses eucharistic symbolism. The central problem is the use of sacrificial language to interpret not only Jesus' death, but also our lives as well. Clearly, such language engages all the problems discussed in the previous chapter with regard to sacrificial interpretations of suffering and implications for women. But more concretely, the body and blood symbolism of the eucharistic bread and wine, as representing a male body and male blood contrasts sharply with the churches' traditional rejection of women's bodies and blood as dangerous and polluting.

Although the rhetoric that surrounds the celebration of the Christian meal appears to emphasize spirituality and unity, and minimize difference and dominance, the politics of eucharistic community influence a set of feminist critiques against traditional eucharistic prayer and practice. The Roman Catholic and Orthodox churches refuse ordination to women and insist on the necessity of ordination for "valid" eucharistic presidency. In the thought of some Latin American liberation theologians, ethical principles must prevail in order for the eucharist to be "valid." Colombian Catholic theologian Rafael Avila makes this argument from the perspective of the struggle for human rights in Latin America:

> We believe that at this historical moment the only legitimate context for the eucharist—a Eucharist such as we have proposed—is only in solidarity with the movement for the liberation of our continent, and more concretely with the exploited classes of our

society. . . . Therefore the only persons qualified to participate in this celebration are those working for liberation, with the understanding that this implies the suppression of the objective conditions that make it possible for some to be exploited and others to be exploiters.[7]

This position, interpreted specifically from the perspective of women, would challenge the "validity" of all eucharistic meals observed in traditional mainstream Christian churches. Since the category of "validity" is a patriarchally defined one, and one which has been/is used most often against women's liturgical agency, this is a strategy of reversal, demonstrating the use of patriarchal categories against patriarchal institutions and practices. In particular, arguments from male church leaders about the "validity" of the ordination of women or of the sacraments they preside over demonstrate the limits of language of validity as a useful way of talking about the Christian meal. In place of A/Not-A thinking (valid/invalid), we must discover or create standards of eucharistic praying that recognize and honor diversity, that empower the disempowered, and that create ritual environments that nurture resistance, survival, and well-being.

Even aside from its use as a means of delegitimating women's liturgical agency, language about validity has focused on increasingly narrow and doctrinal emphases that have worked not only against ritual felicity, but also against communal participation and empowerment. Validity is defined and interpreted by male, normally clerical, ritual experts, rather than by the participation of the community or by the effectiveness of the ritual event.

Although of late the eucharistic liturgy in general and its prayer in particular have been the focus of considerable discussion among liturgical scholars, the issues under consideration in those conversations generally take account only of the feminist critique of the liturgical use of exclusive language. Concern for this issue has in fact motivated the creation of new prayers and ritual in several North American denominations. The Presbyterian *Worshipbook*, published in 1972, used contemporary English, but "was markedly sexist."[8] New liturgies were composed immediately, and published first as trial liturgies in *Service for the Lord's Day* and later included in the *Book of Common Worship*. The use of nonsexist language was a general concern of the whole collection, but one prayer in particular was written using nonsexist standards of language usage:

> Neither the people of God nor the deity was referred to by the use of sex-specific words. The word "Father" was avoided, as was the word "Son," although masculine pronouns were used with reference to Christ.[9]

Similarly, the Episcopal church produced *Prayer Book Studies 30*, a collection of supplemental liturgical texts in response to the need for "inclusive-language liturgical texts."[10] This collection includes two eucharistic prayers. These prayers, like those of the Presbyterian books, use non-gender specific language for the community and God. Moreover, they expand the biblical images by focusing on creation in God's image and the goodness of creation in general and employ wisdom imagery, albeit very modestly.[11] However, the more difficult problems, of sacrificial language and the role of Jesus, remain.

A question arises: given these deep difficulties with traditional eucharistic praying, given also the strong (for some) attachment to the eucharistic event, and given the liturgical agency and creativity already discussed as present in feminist prayer groups, how do we account for the absence of collections of feminist eucharistic prayers? Why do accounts of oral feminist liturgies so often lack descriptions of reconceived Christian feminist eucharists? Or is the eucharistic meal so deeply embedded in the churches' patriarchal ordering that it should be abandoned, rejected completely in feminist liturgy, or replaced by other, more emancipatory, rituals? Is this a ritual to which feminists must, at least for the present time, say *no*?

It is my conviction that Christian identity is ritually created, not doctrinally defined, and that at the center of Christian feminist praying is not finally words but objects and action, generating and extending emancipatory life beyond ritual into the political and social world. The eucharistic table has been, as South African biblical scholar Itumeleng Mosala said of the Bible, "the product, the record, the site, and the weapon of class, cultural, gender, and racial struggles."[12] Feminist Christians can no more reject the eucharistic action than we can reject the Bible. But like the Bible, we cannot enshrine the eucharist as received and practiced as if it came from God. We recognize and name its political context, its uses to reinforce the powerful and intimidate and oppress the powerless, indeed to create and maintain structures of dominance and submission that make such oppression possible.

The eucharistic bread has been for centuries, and in most places continues to be, not bread of life for women, but bread of affliction; the cup not of salvation and health but the cup of bitterness. To these oppressive practices we must say *no*. But how can we do so? And can these experiences be ritualized, honored and recognized, in the Christian meal? What resources can be found in Christian practice and in feminist understanding, to create eucharists that nourish us and enable us to resist our own oppression and suffering? As with the Bible, we also claim the table as our table, the rite as our rite, that we are empowered to redefine and reconstruct as necessary to insure our well-being and the well-being of all.

But what shape should such praying take? How does feminist eucharistic praying understand the memorial of Jesus? How does it interpret Jesus' life and death, or does it? How does it enact the meal, as ritual and nourishment? What place does giving thanks hold in feminist meal prayers?

In order to consider these questions, we will first examine the theological questions and issues that have shaped contemporary Christian eucharistic praying, with particular attention to the words of institution and to the idea of sacrifice. Then we will turn to a review of resources for Christian feminist eucharistic praying. Finally we will take up the implications of feminist "prayer in the memory of Jesus" for feminist eucharistic praying.

The Words of Institution

The "words of institution" or "institution narrative" texts have been assumed by the church to present the origin of the eucharist or Lord's Supper. Also called the "Last Supper," these texts are found in four places in the New Testament: Mark 14:22-24; Matthew 26:26-28; I Corinthians 11:23-25; and Luke 22:19-20. The meaning of these words has been the focus of scholarly debate for centuries.[13] Such a focus appears to reinforce the Western medieval exclusive emphasis on these words as consecratory and as definitive in some way. Whereas Roman Catholic eucharistic prayers still assume that these words are consecratory, Protestant eucharistic prayers use them as scriptural warrant or originating narrative. This apologetic focus needs to interpret the scriptural account of the so-called last supper of Jesus as a constitutive event, as the founding meal of Christianity.

From a feminist perspective, the institution texts are problematic. In part this is due, no doubt, to the great prominence given this text in contemporary Western communion rituals and prayers. Not only is it regarded as consecratory by Roman Catholics and necessary warrant by mainline Protestants, but even churches that reject more formal prayer and ritual for the communion meal include at least a reading of one of the institution texts. Moreover, this text has been the locus for denying women's liturgical agency as presider at the eucharistic table. Where these words are interpreted as consecratory or in some other way sacred, then they are the words forbidden to women to say. As the role of presiding at the eucharistic table came to be the basis for hierarchical authority in the church, these words take on the character of a weapon against women's liturgical agency and religious authority.

When feminist students in a class on eucharist attempted to write feminist eucharistic prayers, the element they changed most dramatically was this element. They replaced the institution narrative with the miraculous feeding narrative or the story of Jesus with the woman at the well. Another Protestant feminist resists going to communion services because of discomfort with atonement theologies expressed in the institution narrative, particularly the symbolism of body and blood. Yet another admits that although the newer eucharistic prayers emphasize thanksgiving and praise for the resurrection rather than confession and penitence for the suffering and death, for her the words of institution loom too large over the elements of thankful praise. She does not attend. And another refuses to receive communion if the words "The body of Christ, broken for you," are used at the distribution. These words make suffering and death sacrificial and salvific, and mistake death for life.

Traditional interpretations of the words of institution rely on positivist interpretations of scripture that assume, among other things, that the texts are accurate accounts of the words and actions of Jesus, that the meaning is primarily religious and ritual, rather than political, that the words reflect a historical account of the origins of the Christian meal, and that the central words of the text are "this is my body," "this is my blood," and "do this in remembrance of me." To the extent that these words have been understood as consecratory, or at least sacred in some specialized way, they have been the words forbidden to women. This meal, whether it is understood as a Passover meal or not, is given priority over other meal stories in the Christian scriptures, and over the Johannine account of Jesus' final evening with the disciples, which lacks any institution narrative. It lacks, in its canonical versions, any reference to the presence of women, unlike other meal stories in the New Testament, such as the miraculous feeding narratives, or Jesus' meals with social and religious outcasts, including prostitutes.

Sacrifice in Christian Eucharistic Prayer

There are two issues here that are not always kept distinct in discussions of sacrifice and the eucharist. One issue is whether or not the eucharistic action is best, or even in part, understood as a sacrifice. The second, related issue is whether the death of Jesus is best understood as a sacrifice. In the connection between these two issues lies much of the problem of contemporary eucharistic praying.

Scholars generally agree with William Crockett that "in the New Testament, the eucharist is nowhere explicitly called a sacrifice."[14] New Testament scholar Joanna Dewey observes that "given the ubiquity of sacrifice in the Mediterranean world, it plays a surprisingly small role [in the Second Testament]."[15] In the late-first-century document called the *Didache* the prayers for the meal do not include sacrificial references. However, the author describes the meal event as a sacrifice and employs language of purity and defilement to speak of it:

> On every Lord's Day—his special day—come together and break bread and give thanks, first confessing your sins so that your sacrifice may be pure. Anyone at variance with his neighbor must not join you, until they are reconciled, lest your sacrifice be defiled.[16]

Later Christian writers on the eucharist use sacrificial terminology, which by the third century begins to be included in prayer texts themselves. This sacrificial idea, at first applied metaphorically or typologically to the eucharistic meal, in the Middle Ages was elaborated in detail. The Mass was seen as propitiatory sacrifice: the priest offered sacrifice on behalf of the people, the table became an altar, bread and wine became sacrificial offerings of body and blood. Ideas of purity and defilement were applied to priest, attendants, people, and all materials that came into contact with the sacred Host, "host" meaning, after all, "victim." The reformers objected to this sacrificial ritual economy most strongly, regarding it, in Martin Luther's words, as "a most impious re-crucifying." However, while rejecting the idea of the Mass as a sacrifice, they did not object to the understanding of Jesus' death as sacrificial. This event was the one, sufficient sacrifice that could not and need not be repeated, as the Catholics claimed to do. Although much of the acrimony of the Reformation has dissipated, most Protestant prayers are very cautious about the use of sacrificial language in reference to the eucharist, and even more cautious about its use in prayers.

The second related, but distinct, issue is whether Jesus' death is properly or helpfully (or even accurately) understood as sacrifice. As discussed in the previous chapter, feminist theologians reject traditional interpretations of Jesus' death as salvific, as necessary, or as demanded by God. Yet various expressions of these themes, particularly of the death of Jesus as sacrificial, permeate virtually all contemporary eucharistic prayers. Contemporary commentators on eucharistic prayers locate the problem with the interpretation of the prayer and action as sacrificial, but grant the sacrificial nature of Jesus' death. The Lima document, an ecumenical statement on baptism, eucharist and ministry, makes such a move, defining the eucharist as memorial, but the death of Jesus as sacrificial:

> The eucharist is the memorial of the crucified and risen Christ, i.e. the living and effective sign of his sacrifice, accomplished once and for all on the cross and still operative on behalf of all humankind.[17]

Embedded in every contemporary eucharistic prayer and taken for granted in virtually every analysis of eucharistic praying is the assumption that Jesus' death is best understood as a sacrifice and the eucharistic meal as, in the words of the Lima document, "an effective sign" of that sacrificial death.

However, if, as I argued in the preceding chapter on Jesus, sacrificial interpretations of his suffering and death fail to take seriously his own resistance to his suffering and death and create a symbolic and moral environment that is harmful, how are we to understand the meaning of Jesus' life and death in the eucharistic action? Since the Middle Ages, and even earlier, the meal has been interpreted in sacrificial terms, although not so exclusively as it would seem from contemporary prayers. What other models for eucharistic praying are available? What other models need to be created?

Religious anthropologist Nancy Jay has argued persuasively that practice of sacrifice "remedies having-been-born-of-woman, establishing bonds of intergenerational continuity between males that transcend their absolute dependency on childbearing women."[18] From this sacrificial system, in which the blood of the victim purifies whereas women's menstrual and childbirth blood pollutes, arises hierarchical relationships that confirm patrilineal lineage. In sacrificial systems, childbearing women are not allowed to sacrifice. Jay traced the development of Christian ideas about the eucharist as sacrifice to the second century, as a means of responding to threats from within and without. This "sacrificially maintained social structure" was based on an understanding of the eucharist as the Christian sacrifice and the bishops who presided as "unilineal descendents of the apostles."[19]

Although Jay noted that "nowhere in the New Testament is the eucharist described as being itself a sacrifice,"[20] and acknowledged that first the Reformation and more recently the reforms of Vatican II have disrupted the hegemony of this sacrificial system, she also argued that it is a system that depends on and maintains gender dichotomy and male domination.

It is interesting to note that the theme of sacrifice is most strongly stated in the contemporary eucharistic prayers of the Roman Sacramentary and least strongly stated in prayers of churches that ordain women to the service of the table. Jay observed that Roman Catholic theologian Hans Küng, who advocates the ordination of women to the priesthood, also rejects the sacrificial understanding of the Mass.[21]

However, it would be a mistake to assume that the historic Protestant aversion to referring to the eucharistic rite as a sacrifice means that sacrificial language and symbolism is not present in

Protestant worship. Nothing could be further from the truth. Resistance to the use of sacrificial language to understand the eucharist does not mean refusal to use sacrificial language to understand the death of Jesus, which is memorialized in the communion rite.

In the first place, contemporary Protestant prayers, for the most part, do use some sort of sacrificial language. For example, the standard United Methodist prayer for regular Sunday use, found in the *United Methodist Hymnal*, for congregational use, employs the phrase, "On the night in which he gave himself up for us," to introduce the institution narrative, giving it a sacrificial context. Moreover, the words over the cup, following Matthew's account, and in common with all other contemporary prayers, include the phrase, "blood . . . poured out for you and for many for the forgiveness of sins." This phrase implies expiatory sacrifice. Finally, the invocation of the Spirit prays that "we may be for the world the body of Christ, redeemed by his blood," a phrase that suggests sacrificial atonement.

In the second place, Protestant ritual and belief is expressed as powerfully and importantly in hymnody as in prayer text. And here the sacrificial language comes fully to the fore. Charles Wesley's collection of hymns included a section entitled, "The Holy Eucharist as It Implies a Sacrifice." A Wesley hymn included in the *United Methodist Hymnal*, "Come Sinners to the Gospel Feast," includes the stanza:

> See him set forth before your eyes;
> behold the bleeding sacrifice. . . .[22]

Nineteenth- and early twentieth-century revival hymns, still very popular in many Protestant churches, frequently refer to Jesus' death in sacrificial and redemptive terms:

> Blessed assurance, Jesus is mine!
> O what a foretaste of glory divine!
> Heir of salvation, purchase of God,
> born of his spirit, washed in his blood.[23]

> There is a fountain filled with blood drawn from
>   Emmanuel's veins;
> and sinners plunged beneath that flood lose all their
>   guilty stains.

> Dear dying Lamb, thy precious blood shall never lose its
>   power
> till all the ransomed church of God be saved, to sin no
>   more.[24]
>
> I heard an old, old story, how a Savior came from glory,
> how he gave his life on Calvary to save a wretch like me;
> I heard about his groaning, of his precious blood's atoning,
> then I repented of my sins and won the victory.
> O victory in Jesus, my Savior forever!
> He sought me and bought me with his redeeming blood;
> he loved me ere I knew him, and all my love is due him;
> he plunged me to victory beneath the cleansing flood.[25]

Even where newer hymnals provide celebratory, nonsacrifical hymns for use with new communion rites and prayers emphasizing thanksgiving, these older "blood" hymns continue in popularity and continue to shape the piety and spirituality of worshiping communities and their understanding of the meaning of the memorial of Jesus' death.

Finally, some Protestant traditions that rejected sacrificial language for the eucharistic meal in the sixteenth century have begun to employ it in their prayers. For example, although Lutheran theologian Gordon Lathrop argues that "Christian worship is not sacrifice,"[26] he nevertheless concludes that it is necessary for churches and liturgies to continue to use the term sacrifice:

> . . . Given the importance of this language in the tradition and the perdurance to our own day of the human interest in holy gift and holy violence as a compelling link with deity, we should maintain the language, even increase its use, but do so with a fierce insistence on breaking and converting its power.[27]

In a similar vein, writing of the eucharistic prayers in the *Lutheran Book of Worship*, Gail Ramshaw argues that "it is no longer defensible for Lutherans to continue their eccentric refusal to speak the language of offering and sacrifice in the eucharist."[28]

However, as Jay also observed, the decline of the importance of sacrifice as a means of social control in an individualistic, technological society does not necessarily spell liberation for women: "There is more than one way to exclude women from control of the production of religious meaning."[29] Sacrificial language, even when used metaphorically as it is in the eucharist (at

127

least so argues Gordon Lathrop), may no longer function to maintain patrilineal descent, but in an individualist society marked by gender dichotomy, it still serves to reinforce patriarchal values of female submission, suffering, altruism, and self-sacrifice.

Issues in Contemporary Eucharist Prayers

Contemporary reforms of Christian eucharistic prayer provide an ambiguous resource for feminist eucharistic praying. On the one hand, much of the direction of liturgical reform has been retrograde, an attempt to recover ancient practices and understandings under the assumption that these are superior to more recent practices. Although the "older is better" paradigm has begun to be challenged by more refined historical method, current reforms still demonstrate a preference for patterns understood to be ancient. At the same time, however, the same historical recovery that has fueled this retrograde movement in liturgical reform has also provided much of the information that challenges some of the liturgical practices most criticized by feminists. Thus from a feminist perspective, while the churches' liturgical practices of the past cannot serve as an uncriticized model for contemporary emancipatory praying, emancipatory elements from past practice can resource an emancipatory model.

Contemporary reform of Christian eucharistic praying began with the publication of new eucharistic prayers for use in the Roman Catholic Church after the Second Vatican Council. Before these reforms, the standard eucharistic practice in both Catholic and Protestant churches was the use of a single eucharistic prayer (although some Protestant churches did not, and some still do not, use a prayer at all, but instead recite or read the institution narrative). These single prayers reflected the theological interpretations of each tradition, but they had in common a late-medieval focus on the passion and death of Jesus and on penitence as as the proper worshipful attitude. In addition, these prayers generally lacked significant reference to the work of the Holy Spirit or to eschatological hope and expectation. Jesus' death was the focus, and the interpretation of that death was the focus of the major controversies of the Reformation still reflected in the prayers.

Reforms changed much of this practice. Multiple prayers were produced in place of the single prayer; the prayer was recast as thanksgiving instead of penitence; the content was expanded to include reference to the life, resurrection, and anticipated coming again of Christ instead of only his passion. Perhaps the most decisive change had to do with the virtually unanimous adoption of the "Antiochene" pattern for the prayer itself. This prayer moves from general thanksgiving and praise to the institution narrative, followed by an explicit statement of remembrance of Christ, an invocation of the Spirit, intercessions (sometimes), and a concluding doxology. The following chart demonstrates the basic shape of the prayer and gives a contemporary example, this one from the *United Methodist Hymnal* (p. 9ff.):

Opening dialogue: establishes the purpose of the prayer as thanksgiving and the presider's authority to offer the prayer on behalf of the assembled congregation.	The Lord be with you. **And also with you.** Lift up your hearts. **We lift them up to the Lord.** Let us give thanks to the Lord our God. **It is right to give our thanks and praise.**
Preface: offers thanks to God, typically by recounting salvation history, sometimes by recalling particular acts of God in the case of seasonal or occasional prayers.	It is right, and a good and joyful thing, always and everywhere to give thanks to you, Father Almighty, creator of heaven and earth. You formed us in your image and breathed into us the breath of life. When we turned away, and our love failed, your love remained steadfast. You delivered us from captivity, made covenant to be our sovereign God, and spoke to us through your prophets. And so, with your people on earth and all the company of heaven, we praise your name and join their unending hymn:
Sanctus and *benedictus qui venit*: congregational scriptural song of praise.	**Holy, holy, holy Lord, God of power and might, heaven and earth are full of your glory. Hosanna in the highest. Blessed is he who comes in the name of the Lord. Hosanna in the highest.**

Post-*Sanctus*: continuation of the thanksgiving, usually focusing on the work of Jesus.

Holy are you, and blessed is your son Jesus Christ.
Your Spirit anointed him to preach good news to the poor, to proclaim release to the captives and recovering of sight to the blind, to set at liberty those who are oppressed, and to announce that the time had come when you would save your people.
He healed the sick, fed the hungry, and ate with sinners.
By the baptism of his suffering, death, and resurrection you gave birth to your church, delivered us from slavery to sin and death,and made with us a new covenant by water and the Spirit.
When the Lord Jesus ascended, he promised to be with us always, in the power of your Word and Holy Spirit.

Institution Narrative: recounts the institutional words of the "last supper," traditionally not quoted directly from scripture, but often a conflation of accounts.

On the night in which he gave himself up for us, he took bread, gave thanks to you, broke the bread, gave it to his disciples, and said,
"Take, eat; this is my body which is given for you.
Do this in remembrance of me."
When the supper was over, he took the cup, gave thanks to you, gave it to his disciples, and said:
"Drink from this, all of you; this is my blood of the new covenant, poured out for you and for many for the forgiveness of sins.
Do this, as often as you drink it, in remembrance of me."

Anamnesis and oblation: a declaration of remembrance of Jesus together with a declaration of offering of some kind: of congregation, of praise, of bread and wine.

And so, in remembrance of these your mighty acts in Jesus Christ, we offer ouselves in praise and thanksgiving as a holy and living sacrifice, in union with Christ's offering for us, as we proclaim the mystery of faith.

Memorial acclamation: a congregational song.

Christ has died; Christ is risen; Christ will come again.

Epiclesis: invocation of the Holy Spirit on the gifts and sometimes

Pour out your Holy Spirit on us gathered here, and on these gifts of

	bread and wine.
on the congregation also.	Make them be for us the body and blood of Christ, that we may be for the world the body of Christ, redeemed by his blood.
	By your Spirit make us one with Christ, one with each other, and one in ministry to all the world, until Christ comes in final victory and we feast at his heavenly banquet.
Doxology: final trinitarian praise; this example follows the text of Hippolytus' *Apostolic Tradition* with its reference to "holy church"; other formulations are also used.	Through your Son Jesus Christ, with the Holy Spirit in your holy church, all honor and glory is yours, almighty Father, now and forever.
Congregational amen.	**Amen.**

The translation of the Roman Canon into English (and other vernacular languages) was accompanied by the creation of three new eucharistic prayers, based on ancient patterns. The new prayers, departing from the Roman pattern, follow the Antiochene pattern of prayer. This pattern, rather than the Roman canon, has become the predominant form adopted subsequently in Protestant eucharistic reform, even though other patterns can be found in historic documents. One consequence of this widespread acceptance of the Antiochene pattern is a high degree of convergence among the various denominational versions of the eucharistic prayer.[30]

All contemporary prayers make it clear that the medieval-Reformation emphasis on the prayer as a commemoration or reenactment of the passion of Jesus is inadequate. Recovery of the Antiochene pattern with its developed preface full of thanksgiving and praise, as well as a clearer understanding of the celebratory character of early eucharistic prayers, has fueled that shift. That shift has concurrently reduced emphasis on the penitential character of the previous prayers. It has also meant expanding references in the prayer to the life and ministry of Jesus, rather than focusing solely on his suffering and death, as do older prayers. The resurrection is more prominent as well. Eschatological hope, an aspect long absent from eucharistic prayers in the Western churches, receives more emphasis, as does the work of the Spirit. Furthermore, contemporary prayers, particularly some of the newest ones, attempt to address contemporary environmental concerns by expanding the content of the thanksgiving to include thanksgiving for creation and acknowledgment of our place in that good creation.

While much of the impetus of the liturgical movement has been retrograde, seeking to recover and restore ancient patterns, scholars now generally agree that the search for a single original pattern for Christian eucharistic praying is fruitless. However, as in the case of reconsideration of some primitive meanings of prayer in the name of Jesus, a brief examination of elemental strata in Christian eucharistic praying may help free contemporary prayer from some of its more problematic assumptions.

In the first place, it must be said that Christian eucharistic praying has been, until the sixteenth century, marked by diversity and multiformity.[31] Contemporary reforms seem to acknowledge this, even while attempting to limit or control "authorized" prayer texts. The Roman Catholic Sacramentary provides four different prayers for general use, two for children, and two for services of reconciliation (where it formerly had only one). The Episcopal *Book of Common Prayer* provides four different texts and a form for *ex tempore* eucharistic prayer (where former Prayer Books only included one). The United Methodist Church has produced a series of collections of eucharistic prayers, culminating in 21 different prayers in the *Book of Worship*, although the *United Methodist Hymnal* includes only two texts. The Presbyterian *Book of Common Worship* provides eight different prayers, where earlier books offered only a single model. The *Lutheran Book of Worship* offers four prayers, although the pew edition provides only one of these.

Second, the meal character of the eucharist is emphasized over sacrificial act or dramatic reenactment of the passion. This invites the decentering of the "Last Supper"/institution narrative emphasis by reiteration of other meal stories about Jesus, such as the miraculous feedings, with their eschatological themes, the messianic banquet parables, and Jesus' scandalous meals with outcasts. However, although some contemporary prayers refer in passing to these meals, the institution narrative, with its focus on the death of Jesus, remains central in all prayers, due to the almost unvarying acceptance of the Antiochene structure. Only the Presbyterian collection includes prayers without the institution narrative in the prayer itself, although the words are to be recited outside the prayer, usually at the breaking of the bread, as a credal statement.[32]

Third, the recovery of the Jewish roots of Christian eucharist in Jewish meal prayers has meant a recovery of the Christian meal as thanksgiving, rather than as the confession or penitence it had become in the Middle Ages, and as it carried over into the liturgies of the Reformation. Particularly in the opening section of the Antiochene prayer pattern, the preface, God is thanked and blessed by means of a recitation of salvation history. Thus, in this prayer form, the commemoration of the death of Jesus is located in a context of thanksgiving and praise. Catholic liturgical scholar David Power notes the limitations of this approach: "When there is a sharp contrast beween God's deeds of old and any present calamity, thanksgiving is not enough to express the covenant relationship between God and people."[33] He argues for including, within thanksgiving, lament and complaint against God and against one's enemies.

Resources for a Feminist Emancipatory Theology of Suffering

"Let this cup pass from me. . . ."(Matthew 26:39)

Although it is clear that the political and hierarchical context in which the eucharist is celebrated is deeply problematic for women, the central problem with the prayer itself is its dependence (in spite of contemporary reforms) on sacrificial language and imagery. Sacrificial rhetoric, however nuanced or reinterpreted, is an inadequate understanding of the meaning of suffering. In rejecting sacrificial language, feminist theology does not deny the reality of suffering; instead, it rejects any understanding of suffering that diminishes the possibility of resistance and struggle.

David Power suggests that "exhortations to patience and submission seem to have muted" expressions of lament or complaint in Christian prayer.[34] Such exhortations, of course, depend on sacrificial rhetoric, as do exhortations to submission and acceptance of suffering. Sheila Redmond identifies three ways in which Christian culture has valued suffering: as punishment for sin (either actual or inherited), as teaching of humility, and as an opportunity for martyrdom. Jesus, of course, is interpreted in parts of the New Testament and other Christian writings as a martyr (Revelation 1:5; the Greek word *martyr* is usually translated "witness" in this text). Redmond goes on to demonstrate how this valuing of suffering (as well as other related Christian virtues, such as forgiveness, sexual purity, need for redemption, and odedience to authority) hampers recovery from child sexual abuse.[35] In fact, such valuing also hampers resistance against all forms of suffering and violence.

Instead of valuing suffering, feminist theology proposes alternative responses to suffering. These responses include resistance, community, remembrance, and valuation of the body. In place of sacrifice, resistance to suffering; in place of the solitary martyr, the community of resistors; in place of denial of the costs of sacrifice and martyrdom, naming and remembrance; in place of willing sacrifice of the body, loving and honoring the body in all its diverse forms, human and nonhuman.

Feminist Meals and Feminist Fasts

If the prevailing sacrificial orientation of traditional eucharistic theology is problematic from feminist perspectives, what resources for feminist ritual meals are available from feminist practice? The most commonly invoked resource is based on a revaluing of women's traditional connection with meal preparation and meal sharing.

For a class ritual, two women students planned a meal ritual.[36] Class members waited in the hall while the room, not our usual classroom, was prepared. At last we were invited in. The usually sterile room was now transformed into a dining room: tables were drawn together and covered with linen table cloths. Around the large central tables were four smaller tables, one in each corner of the room. Each of the smaller tables held candles, colorful napkins, food, serving dishes, and small objects such as shells, colorful stones, fresh-cut flowers, and strings of beads.

The two hosts, attired in aprons, ushered us in and invited us to take our places at the table, where we were divided into four groups. Each group was responsible for preparing one of the four courses of the meal at one of the side tables. One group prepared a salad with the greens, fresh vegetables, and dressing provided.

Another group mixed together the ingredients for a tabouli salad. A large loaf of bread was sliced and artistically prepared on a platter; and ingredients for ice cream sundaes were readied.

The hosts then invoked each course and its preparers. The members of each group presented their course to the central table in turn, with solemnity or hilarity, bringing also the lighted candles from the smaller tables, and selected small objects, to adorn the dining table. The dining table was soon full of flickering candles, shells, stones, glittering beads, and fresh flowers. As the dishes were passed and the meal begun, the hosts invited reflections on significant meals. Stories of learning to cook, of special family holiday dinners, of failures or successfully disguised failures, emerged. The candles burned down, the food was consumed, but still we lingered, unwilling to break the mood. At last the final blessing was pronouced by the hosts, and just as all had helped to prepare the meal and the table, all helped clean up and return the room to its former state.

The discussion of this ritual the following week focused on the way the class members began to see that their meals with women friends, sisters, and family were part of their necessary spiritual nurture. They perceived aprons as liturgical garments, food and table preparation as sacred ritual activity. Spontaneous ritual, storytelling, and use of objects from traditional female culture reshaped their understanding of meals.

From the resources of women's traditional meal-centered culture come new possibilities for ritual meals, or perhaps a discovery of rituals that were always there but rendered invisible and marginal by patriarchal ritual. The gathering of women in the kitchen, the laughter and common work of preparing food, the setting of the table, with attention to color and light, to texture and atmosphere, the attention to gracious hospitality, are the elements used by these students in constructing their ritual.

Yet if we stop there we follow patriarchal patterns in seeing only the beauty and not the pain, in hearing only the laughter and not the weeping, only the plenty and not the want. When we valorize, by ritual, the traditional women's work of meal preparation and presentation, we must also recognize the context of exploitation and control, of violence and abuse, of assumption of privilege and entitlement in which these meals take place.

This is a place where class and race complicate gender dichotomy. Not only is meal preparation and presentation a gendered activity ("women's work"); it is also the work of poor or immigrant women and sometimes men. The exploitation of the labor of women of color, of poor women, of "foreign" women, is most clearly expressed here. And the exploiter in such contexts and history, at least in the Western world, is the privileged white woman. Feminist appropriation of meal ritual for eucharistic reconception must take account of this context. Indeed, this context may demand not meal but fast, a ritual *no* to exploitive consumption. This proposal expands on the feminist eucharistic fast that refuses to participate in eucharists that deny liturgical and moral agency to women. It recognizes that the patriarchal system not only creates contexts in which men are permitted to do harm to women, but in which women who enjoy patriarchal privilege may do harm to other women. What is needed in light of this reality is a feminist fast of eucharists that exploit race and class divisions among women.

Engendering Feminist Eucharistic Praying

What shape must feminist eucharistic praying take? What kind of meals, what kind of remembrances are necessary for our ongoing nourishment and well-being? And how can Christian resources and feminist resources be brought together for the engendering of ritual?

Drawing from the earliest eucharistic practices of Christian gatherings, and following the developments of contemporary eucharistic praying, feminist eucharistic praying must be diverse and take many different forms. Feminist eucharistic praying will be diverse not only in content but also in the forms used and the purposes intended.

Thanksgiving alone will not be a sufficient form to hold the possible meanings of meals for feminist gatherings. Some prayers must be made to hold bitterness and betrayal, to ritualize the suffering and struggle of women without the necessity of giving thanks. To demand an attitude of thanks from those who are justly angry and bitter is to disrespect their suffering. Such prayers may follow the pattern of some of the psalms: complaining to God for God's failures, for God's absence; lamenting all that has been lost. These meals will not be eucharists ("thanksgivings"),

136

but meals of sorrow, a ritual eating of the bread of betrayal and drinking from the cup of bitterness, in acknowledgment of the unredeemed sorrow and suffering in the world.[37]

A mourning meal. To be observed in times of great suffering and loss. Let the bread be dry and tasteless, stale. Let the cup be filled with bitter wine, or vinegar, or salt water. Let the participants bring non-musical noisemakers: rattles, drums, ratchets and the like, to wake up God.

May God hear our cry.
May God read the signs of our hearts.
Bring your complaints before God.
We bring our sorrows and accusations.

O God, you have promised to be with us, but you have hidden your face;
you have called and claimed us as your own, but you have let our enemies triumph over us.
Where were you, O God, when we needed you?
When Jephtha murdered his daughter in payment to you, where were you?
Where were you, O God, when we needed you?
When the Levite's concubine was raped and murdered and dismembered, where were you?
Where were you, O God, when we needed you?
When Tamar was raped by her brother, where were you?
Where were you, O God, when we needed you?
. . . .
[Here let members of the assembly name their complaints against God, in direct address to God. To each complaint, let all respond:]
Where were you, O God, when we needed you?
[after final complaint, a leader says:]
Together with the suffering and the oppressed, the raped and the

In place of the traditional opening dialogue, emphasizing the rightness of thanks and praise, this dialogue authorizes the bringing of sorrow and complaints before God.

In place of traditional recounting of God's mighty deeds, here God's failures are named. The biblical examples may be added to, by inclusion of additional biblical examples, and by addition of contemporary examples, such as the persecution of witches, the institution of slavery in North America, the Holocaust, and so on. The list may conclude with individual complaints.

betrayed, the battered and the murdered, we cry:

**Because of you we are being killed all day long,
and accounted as sheep for the slaughter.
Rouse yourself! Why do you sleep, O God?**

In place of the scriptural song of praise, the *Sanctus* and *Benedictus*, is this cry from Psalm 44:22-23. While saying these words, the participants may sound their noisemakers.

Jesus too knew betrayal and abandonment.
On the night he was betrayed by his friends and abandoned to suffering and death, Jesus took the bread of betrayal, prayed to you, and gave it to them, saying:
"Take, eat; this is my body. Whenever you do this, remember me."
Then he took the cup of bitterness, prayed to you, and
shared it with them, saying:
"Drink this, all of you. This is my blood, poured out. Whenever you do this, remember me."

This version of the institution narrative focuses on Jesus' bitterness and sense of betrayal.

In remembrance of all the forgotten, abandoned, and neglected ones, we share this bread of betrayal and cup of bitterness. All those you have forgotten, we remember in this bread and this cup. We remember too that in raising Jesus from the dead you refused his death. Refuse our suffering and death and the suffering of all who are now abandoned by you.

This anamnesis lacks an oblation, since there can be no acceptable offering in place of all who have suffered and continue to suffer far from God. Instead, remembrance, and reminding God, is foremost.

**Why do you hide your face?
Why do you forget our affliction and oppression?**

Another congregational hymn from Psalm 44:24. Noisemakers.

Awake, O God, and remember us. Send us your Spirit. Come to our help and to the help of all who suffer and call on you.

This invocation of the Spirit asks for help. It is not an invocation on the bread and cup, which remain stale and bitter.

**Rise up, come to our help.
Save us for the sake of your steadfast love.**

Psalm 44:26, with noisemakers. The reference to "steadfast love," quoted from the psalm, is somewhat ironic here.

Amen.

But also necessary, and fitting more easily into the thanksgiving pattern, are meals of remembrance and resistance. These ritual meals must involve the recollection of acts of resistance to suffering, including, but not limited to, Jesus' own resistance. These meals will take as their institution narrative not Jesus' last supper but his struggle in the Garden. These prayers will include thanksgiving and lament, remembrance and resistance, desire and fulfillment, hope and emancipation. *A prayer of resistance and demand for justice, in eschatological hope*:

May God hear our cry. **May God read the signs of our hearts.** Bring your desires before God. **We bring our struggles and our demand for justice.**	The opening dialogue confirms the desire for justice, and the right of the community to demand justice from God.
It is right, God of justice, to bring our demands before you. Your steadfast love extends to the heavens, your faithfulness to the clouds. Your righteousness is like the mighty mountains, O God; your judgements are like the great deep; you save humans and animals alike. Yet still our enemies pursue us, O God. Defend us! **How long, O God, will you look on? Rescue us now!** They lay traps for us; foil their plans! **How long, O God, will you look on? Rescue us now!** [Here let participants name their struggles for justice and resistance against suffering. All may respond to each petition with the phrase,] **How long, O God, will you look on? Rescue us now!** [At the conclusion to the individual petitions, a leader may say:] Together with all who resist suffering and oppression, we cry out:	The preface follows the traditional thanksgiving pattern, reminding God that justice and steadfastness are expected. The phrases are taken from Psalms 36 and 35.
You have seen, O God; do not be silent! **O God, do not be far from us!**	In place of the *Sanctus* and *Benedictus*, this cry for deliverance from Psalm 35 and Luke 18:3, the

Wake up! Bestir yourself for our defense, and vindicate us now! Grant us justice against our opponents!

widow's demand to the unjust judge is recalled.

When Jesus went among us, he taught his friends to pray to you for deliverance and to cry to you for justice day and night.
He healed the sick, relieved suffering, raised the dead to life, and promised release to the captives and freedom to the oppressed.

Jesus is remembered as a model of resistance to suffering, pain, and death.

When he saw suffering and death ahead of him, he shared a meal with his friends, blessing bread and cup. After the meal, he took three of his friends and went apart to pray in his fear and grief. He lifted his hands to you and prayed,
"Abba, for you all things are possible. Remove this cup from me."
How long, O God, will you look on? Rescue us now!
And again, after finding his friends asleep, he turned to you again and prayed,
"Abba, for you all things are possible. Remove this cup from me."
How long, O God, will you look on? Rescue us now!
And a third time, his friends slept again, and he went away again and prayed,
"Abba, for you all things are possible. Remove this cup from me."
How long, O God, will you look on? Rescue us now!

In place of the institution narrative, an account of Jesus' resistance to his own suffering is given. The meal becomes a preface to (and anticipation of?) his grief and resistance in the Garden of Gethsemane.

Remembering Jesus' resistance to his own suffering and death, we proclaim the resurrection and persist in demanding justice. May this bread of betrayal become for us the bread of life. May this cup of suffering become for us the cup of freedom.

Resurrection is here identified not with death but with resistance to death. The bread and cup, connected in the institution narrative with betrayal and suffering, are transformed into signs of life and freedom by resistance to suffering and demands for justice.

Send your Holy Spirit on us in anger and power. Sustain our resistance, strengthen our courage, and

The invocation calls the spirit to empower our resistance, which requires anger and courage.

deliver us from the hand of our
enemies.
**How long, O God, will you look
on? Rescue us now!**
Amen.

The congregational refrain from
Psalm 35 concludes the prayer.

Is there no room for thanksgiving prayers in feminist praying?
Can feminists celebrate eucharist? Yes, I believe so. Here is an
example written for a community celebration of women's
ministries.[38]

May God be with you.
And also with you.
Lift up your hearts.
We lift them to our God.
Let us give thanks to God our Help.
**It is right to give our thanks and
praise.**

Holy One of Blessing,
we give you thanks for the lives
and ministries of women:
for those who have gone before us,
breaking new trails,
and for those who stand beside us,
giving us strength for the journey.
**For all faithful women, we give
you thanks and praise.**
In our creation and through the wa-
ters of baptism
you have called us by name.
We give you thanks for that call
and for that naming,
even as we lament our loss:
the loss of the names of our foresis-
ters in the faith;
the loss of their stories of call and
commitment; the loss of their ministries through rejection, betrayal,
and suppression;
distortion, erasure, and silence.
**If we do not speak, let the very
stones cry out!**
Like our sisters before us, we give
you thanks above all for the gift of
your beloved child Jesus.
He too knew rejection, conflict, and
suppression.

The opening dialogue is celebrative
and invites thanksgiving.

The preface gives thanks for
women's ministries (including our
own), but also recognizes and
names our losses. In this service,
emphasis was on the lack of
women's call stories in the gospels.
Another setting might suggest emphasis on more contemporary
losses. We also remember that Jesus
experienced rejection and misun-
derstanding in his ministry. The
congregational acclamation is from
Luke 19:40. At the distribution of
communion, participants also received a small "speaking stone."

His ministry too has been distorted, his gospel of liberation silenced. **If we do not speak, let the very stones cry out!**

For on the night in which he was betrayed by his friends, Jesus took bread, gave you thanks, and said, "Take and eat; whenever you do this, remember me."
And likewise he took the cup, saying, "This is the new covenant; remember me."
If we do not speak, let the very stones cry out!

The words of institution interpret Jesus' death as due to a betrayal rather than self-willed sacrifice. Accordingly, sacrificial language over bread and cup is restricted.

Remembering Jesus, therefore, and remembering the women who bear witness to him, we offer these gifts of bread and wine and ourselves, giving you thanks that in spite of betrayal and silence and death you brought forth hope and life and power.

This section is notable for the phrase "in spite of" which replaces the more traditional phrase "out of." It makes it clear that life is not a result of suffering and death.[39]

Send the power of your strong Spirit on these gifts and on us who are gathered here. Empower us to break the silence, to tell and hear our stories, to live in the struggle for the fulfillment of hope and the restoration of all things, so that in all things we may give you praise and thanksgiving through your child Jesus Christ, with your holy and strong Spirit, now and always.
Amen.

The spirit is invoked for the power to speak, and ongoing thanksgiving is made contingent on the fulfillment of this request.

These three prayers are a mere beginning. They do not exhaust the possibilities for reconceived meal prayers. Banquet prayers for joyful meals; meals without bread and cup, as fasting prayers to acknowledge hungry women, women whose labor is exploited, women unable to feed their children; eucharistic feasts to celebrate our joys and victories, to honor Mary and Martha, or the woman who prophetically anoints Jesus' head before his death, or other biblical or historic or living women.

WISE AS SERPENTS, INNOCENT AS DOVES
Strategies for Feminist Emancipatory Prayer

The language of feminist liturgical prayer is still evolving. Within the borders of established churches, feminist groups are mining their traditions for emancipatory resources, piecing together new forms of prayers out of scraps of the old. Beyond the borders of established churches, feminist groups are engendering new forms of prayer out of ancient religions and feminist awareness. Both types of groups are drawing on what we know as women, of bodies and communities and struggle and change.

The process of claiming the power to create new ways of praying is full of risks. The obvious risks are of being misunderstood and misinterpreted, of being attacked for heresy, of being further marginalized by those who desire to protect the status quo, of being rejected or dismissed as irrelevant. For feminists within or without the established churches, these are familiar risks.

But there are other, less obvious, risks as well. Privileged white women risk replicating in the process and content of prayer the classist and racist practices that benefit us. All women's groups run the risk of trading religious, social, and political transformation for our personal spiritual comfort.

What strategies can help us negotiate these and other risks, determine which risks are worth taking, and create prayer that both comforts and challenges us, and provides the spiritual seedbed of transformation? Here are some suggestions.

Feminist groups must attend both to survival needs and to long-term strategies. As I have already argued, the strategy of "praying between the lines," although useful and even necessary at times, is not in itself transformative. Yet survival is a first value: spiritual, physical, and emotional survival at times may depend on such encoded prayer. But as a long-term strategy, it will only sustain, not change. And it is change that is necessary to our survival in the long run.

Similarly, feminist prayer or ritual groups that attend only to fulfillment of the participants' spiritual needs will function only as a kind of spiritual safety valve, protecting the larger church institutions from having to address the issues raised by women claiming the religious authority to shape their own prayer and ritual. Feminist prayer and ritual groups need to have a double edge. Not only must they attend to their own spiritual needs for nourishment, celebration, and recognition; they must also create the conditions for resistance and transformation. Feminist prayer groups must become communities of strategy, where prayer and ritual not only can be experimented with in new forms and languages, but also can be evaluated, critiqued, and reformed.

Feminist groups must cultivate a practice of self-criticism and ongoing reform. Self-critique is never easy, and the practice of it may feel as if it runs counter to our need for survival strategies of support, encouragement, and empowerment. But it is in the development of such a practice that feminist groups can confront the intersection of various oppressions, including attention to race, class, age, ability, and sexual identity. The risk of the development of a practice of self-criticism and reform is that it will duplicate patriarchal norms of critique. Thus it is essential that each group create its own (always revisable) feminist criteria for evaluation. These criteria might include: shared leadership, remembrance of women's stories, accessibility, disruption of dichotomous categories, respect for the nonhuman world, attention to differing political contexts of participants, and so on.[1]

Feminist prayer must respect differences in women's religious traditions. First and foremost, white Christian feminists must resist appropriating religious practices from other religions. This is always a temptation, since other people's religions usually seem much better than our own. But white Western Christianity has a shameful history of banning, disrupting, demonizing, and exterminating other religious practices, particularly Jewish and Native American. Imitation is not always the sincerest form of flattery; sometimes it is ritual theft.

What this means for feminist prayer, I think, is that we must work at recovering whatever woman-centered traditions and practices we can within our own Christian and cultural traditions. We must also work at making use of the usable parts of our own varied traditions to construct a prayer tradition that enables us to survive and thrive, without doing harm to women of other religious traditions.

By this emphasis on developing distinctively Christian feminist prayer, I do not mean that insularity from other religious traditions is a value. Many feminist prayer groups are already interreligious and appropriately explore the riches of the different religions represented, discovering both commonality and difference. I do mean, however, that historic patterns of oppression, still operative among us, cannot be ignored. In particular, white feminist Christian groups should learn as much as possible about women's lives in other religious groups, ideally from women of those groups directly. But seeking knowledge does not entitle one to plunder these religious traditions for one's own purposes.

A deeper understanding, for example, of the roots of Christian anti-Judaism is essential for a feminist interpretation of Jesus, and therefore for the development of Christian feminist prayer in the name of Jesus. Similarly, an understanding of the ways in which white North American Christians treated Native American religions will help feminist Christians understand the protective privacy that surrounds many contemporary Native American prayer traditions.

Feminist groups must value rather than apologize for their women-only character. As Alice Walker says in defining womanist, separatism is necessary "periodically, for health."[2] For some women, separatism may be a permanent choice; for others, it may be occasional; but for all, it is necessary and healthy. In arguing this, I am not arguing from a female or feminine essentialism. That is, I do not encourage separatism because women are essentially different from men (this argument sustains male-female dichotomous thinking), but because in patriarchal society women are treated differently from men.

An all-women gathering does not leave patriarchy behind, as if we were somehow immune from its effects. But it does give us the possibility for creating a noncoercive space for countering patriarchal ordering. It disrupts patriarchal relationships, which value women's ties with men, by giving priority to women's ties with women. Many women, on discovering the power and joy available to them among women, are all the more pained by the evidence of patriarchy among women. But this is dangerously naive. Women are not innately "better," "more communal," or "more supportive" than men, although we may have learned such skills as survival mechanisms. The struggle to divest ourselves of the ill effects of patriarchy is ongoing. But by giving priority to relationships with women in a women-only group, we can deal with the pains and oppressions we inflict on each other, issues that are often masked in contexts in which our energy goes into caring for or defending ourselves against men.

Feminist groups must claim the liturgical center of their tradition. From the noncoercive, mutually supportive, self-critical space of feminist groups, participants must determine for themselves what aspects of their tradition are valuable and useful, and what aspects should be composted (recycled) or discarded. I have presented in these pages several liturgical elements I believe can be recycled, and several that must be discarded. But each group must determine for itself what elements it values and wishes to preserve in some form, and which must be set aside. It may be that some liturgical practices must be discarded for a time, to be taken up later when the context has changed. The development of criteria for this ongoing process (akin to cleaning out one's closet, I suppose) is also the task of the group.

I have argued here and elsewhere that women must move to the center of their religious traditions, claiming the right and responsibility to shape their central liturgical practices. From a broad historical perspective, those central Christian liturgical elements are proclamation of the word, baptism, and communion. However, local traditions may emphasize one or another of these over the others, or even emphasize other elements, such as foot-washing. Wherever the center of a group's prayer tradition lies, it is there women are most likely to be banned, and there feminist groups must lay claim.

Feminist prayer must enact resistance and dissent, anger,

and grief. Because the practices of resistance, dissent, anger, and grief are so ritually unfamiliar to us, feminist prayer must enable us to rehearse these practices. Thankfulness, celebration, repentance, and guilt are all well-rehearsed in Christian liturgical contexts. Acquiescence and humility are deeply embedded in traditional Christian prayer. But it is strategies of resistance and dissent, expressions of anger and grief, that we need in order to survive over the long term.

In the short term, these practices may well feel disruptive and distressing. As in the development of critical evaluation of feminist prayer, the expression of these modes of behavior in prayer may feel threatening to feminist solidarity. If patriarchal patterns are duplicated, anger and resistance may be displaced. But the development of feminist criteria will help direct the anger and resistance appropriately.

Feminist prayer must develop a vocabulary for lament. Lament in the psalms is not limited to a bewailing of one's sufferings; it also often includes a complaint against God. I have proposed one model for feminist lament in the table prayer of bitterness in Chapter Six. I chose the communion setting, with its traditional memorial of the death of Jesus, in order to claim that Christian lament must include this death, traditionally glorified and spiritualized. Although laments over the death of Jesus are traditionally part of the Good Friday liturgy, the death is interpreted there as necessary, willing, and sacrificial. The prayer of bitterness resists this reading, and thus opens the way to resist our own and others' sufferings and deaths.

But other patterns are also possible. For example, an annual liturgy of lament for the unnecessary deaths of women might be observed each December 6 to commemorate the fourteen women murdered by a lone gunman in a classroom in Montreal. This practice is already suggested in the story of Jephtha's daughter's retreat with her women companions before her death:

So there arose an Israelite custom that for four days every year the daughters of Israel would go out to lament the daughter of Jephtha the Gileadite. (Judges 11:39b-40)

Feminist prayer must develop a vocabulary for anger. As suggested in foregoing chapters, ritual expression of anger is located primarily in curses. The following suggests some ground rules for curses. And what of cursing God?

> handle curses as you would a deadly weapon
>> shining blade, gray gunbarrel
> with care
> with practice
> with infinite regret
>
> use curses as you would a dangerous but saving drug
> after careful diagnosis
> in carefully controlled dosage
> when this is the only hope of recovery
> for someone
>
> send curses as you would shoot an arrow from a bow
> take careful aim
> know your target well
> make sure your arrowhead is sharp, your anger true
> then never doubt it will strike its goal
>
> prepare a curse as you would follow a difficult recipe
> measure exactly
> do not substitute ingredients
> and be patient for results

Feminist prayer must develop a vocabulary for rites of exorcism and purification. The following is a suggested nontraditional pattern for an exorcism. I wrote it for individual use, but it might well serve, with appropriate adaptations, for a group. Perhaps a space in a church needs to be cleansed for feminist use?

> the air in the room is red
>> in the face
>> angry condescending furious heartless
> it intimidates the oxygen from the lungs
>> it makes you gasp grasp
> for anything sweet
> for hope
>
> do not enter the room without protection
>
> bring garlic, in long strings, crinkly and pungent,
>> it strengthens the lungs and repels weakness
> bring clean water, cleanly salted, in a clean smooth bowl
>> it purifies and preserves good will
> bring a talisman or two or many
>> objects of beauty or strangeness or wonder

the smooth stone, the feather of the bird
the beloved face recorded
    they are your witnesses

enter the room singing loudly and bringing your
    protection with you
        hang the garlic on the door
        sprinkle the salt water around the walls
            the floor, the windows
                wherever the air is hard to breathe
        place the talisman in the center of the room,
        or in the corners

sing around the room, slinging tears, slinging birthwaters,
    slinging seawater
        I have come to this place
        it is my place and no other
        all evil fly away
        all insult fly away
        all ill will fly away
        all cruelty fly away
        all fear fly away

        I have come to this place
        it is mine and no one else's
        all goodness come in
        all grace come in
        all resistance come in
        all courage come in
        all laughter come in

repeat as necessary until the air fills your lungs
    sweetly
then light candles
burn fragrant leaves
crush sweet herbs and plants
and tell stories of all the good things that will happen
in this room
now that it is yours

It is the ritual of exorcism that moves most clearly from *no* to
yes, from resistance and rejection to affirmation and celebration.
It is a ritual of prayer of hope enacted in time and place of trouble.
And as Christian women, as feminists attempting to pray with
our eyes open, we are always in a time and place of trouble,
always in need of prayers of honesty and hope.

In the Prologue, I suggested that this book is like a recipe collection, concerned with strategy and transformation. What are the ingredients, then, that must go into feminist prayer? And what are the processes that will bring about transformation?

> *loving our no*:
> > in lament, curse, exorcism
> > to prayer except on our own terms and for our own needs
> > to prayer that is coercive or destructive
>
> *discovering our yes*:
> > to woman-centeredness without apology
> > to respect and honor
> > > for each other
> > > for our bodies as they are
> > > for our differences
> > > for the natural world
>
> *centeredness*:
> > in ourselves
> > in the center of our traditions
>
> *and survival*:
> > the cunning wisdom of the serpent
> > the wise innocence of the dove

NOTES

Notes to Prologue

1. In Olga Broumas, *Beginning with O* (New Haven: Yale University Press, 1977), 24.

2. Elisabeth Schüssler Fiorenza, *Jesus: Miriam's Child, Sophia's Prophet: Critical Issues in Feminist Christology* (New York: Continuum, 1994), 10.

Notes to Chapter One

1. bell hooks, *Teaching to Transgress* (New York: Routledge, 1994), 167.

2. See Eileen King, "What is Feminist Prayer?" in *Women at Worship: Interpretations of North American Diversity,* edited by Marjorie Procter-Smith and Janet Walton (Louisville: Westminster/John Knox, 1994).

3. In addition to the articles in Procter-Smith and Walton cited in note 2, see also Marjorie Procter-Smith, *In Her Own Rite: Constructing Feminist Liturgical Prayer* (Nashville: Abingdon Press, 1990) and "The Marks of Feminist Liturgy," *Proceedings of the North American Academy of Liturgy, 1992;* Janet Walton, "Ecclesial and Feminist Blessing: Women as Objects and Subjects of the Power of Blessing," in Mary Collins and David Power, editors, *Blessing and Power* (Edinburgh: T & T Clark, 1985); Charlotte Caron, *To Make and Make Again: Feminist Ritual Thealogy* (New York: Crossroad, 1993); Lesley A. Northup, "Claiming Horizontal Religious Space: Women's Religious Rituals," *Studia Liturgica* 25, no. 1 (1995).

4. On women as preachers, see Carol Norén, *Woman in the Pulpit* (Nashville: Abingdon Press, 1991); Christine M. Smith, *Weaving the Sermon: Preaching in a Feminist Perspective* (Louisville: Westminster/John Knox Press, 1989) and *Preaching as Weeping, Confession, and Resistance: Radical Responses to Radical Evil* (Louisville: Westminster/John Knox Press, 1992). On inclusive language in liturgical texts, see commentaries on any of the recently revised liturgical books of mainline denominations in North America. For the most thorough attempts to address inclusive language issues in biblical texts used in liturgy, see *The Inclusive Language Lectionary* (Readings for Year A, Philadelphia: John Knox Press, 1983; Year B, Atlanta: John Knox Press, 1984 and 1987; Year C, Atlanta: John Knox Press,

1985 and 1988) and Gail Ramshaw and Gordon Lathrop, *Lectionary for the Christian People* (New York: Pueblo Publishing Co., 1986, 1987, 1988).

5. Carolyn Heilbrun, *Writing a Woman's Life* (New York: Ballantine Books, 1988), 18.

6. Don Saliers, *The Soul in Paraphrase: Prayer and the Religious Affections*, Second Edition (Cleveland, OH: OSL Publications, 1980, 1991).

7. Nancy Jay, "Gender and Dichotomy," *Feminist Studies* 7, no. 1 (1981): 44.

8. Jay, 45.

9. *Ibid.*

10. Cyril Richardson, editor, *Early Christian Fathers* (New York: Collier Books, 1970), 171. A comparable dualistic text is also included in an earlier document, "The Letter of Barnabas."

11. *Ibid.*, 173.

12. A. Hamman, editor, *The Paschal Mystery: Ancient Liturgies and Patristic Texts* (Staten Island, NY: Alba House, 1969), 30.

13. *Ibid.*, 38.

14. Richardson, 358.

15. *Ibid.*, 360.

16. Nancy Jay, *Throughout Your Generations Forever: Sacrifice, Religion, and Paternity* (Chicago: University of Chicago Press, 1992), 21.

17. The classic formulation of this fluidity of orthodoxy and heresy is found in Walter Bauer, *Orthodoxy and Heresy in Earliest Christianity* (Philadelphia: Fortress Press, 1971).

18. Helen Hull Hitchcock, editor, *The Politics of Prayer: Feminist Language and the Worship of God* (San Francisco: Ignatius Press, 1992), xxi.

19. See also Allan Bouley, *From Freedom to Formula: The Evolution of the Eucharistic Prayer from Oral Improvisation to Written Texts*, (Washington, DC: Catholic University of America Press, 1981).

20. Jay, "Gender and Dichotomy," 48.

21. Within North American Protestantism there is a strong tradition of ecstatic, pentecostal prayer, including prayer in tongues, that is difficult to regulate. The history of ecstatic, charismatic prayer and its attempted suppression and control is, in a way, the history of Christian prayer.

22. Catharine MacKinnon, *Toward a Feminist Theory of the State*, (Cambridge: Harvard University Press, 1989), xvi.

23. *Ibid.*, 168.

24. *Ibid.*, 194.

25. Janice Raymond, *A Passion For Friends: Toward a Philosophy of Female Affection* (Boston: Beacon Press, 1986), 62.

26. Elisabeth Castelli, "Les Belles Infidèles/Fidelity or Feminism?" *Journal of Feminist Studies in Religion*, 6, no. 2 (Fall 1990): 25.

27. Quoted in bell hooks, 167.

28. Miriam Therese Winter, Adair Lummis, and Alison Stokes, *Defecting in Place: Women Claiming Responsibility for Their Own Spiritual Lives* (New York: Crossroad Press, 1994).

29. *Ibid.*, 155.

30. bell hooks, 175.

31. *Ibid.*, 173–74.

32. Jay, "Gender and Dichotomy," 49–50.

33. Winter, Lummis, and Stokes, 157.

34. Jay, "Gender and Dichotomy," 54.

35. Ronald Grimes, *Reading, Writing, and Ritualizing* (Washington, DC: The Pastoral Press, 1993), 16.

36. MacKinnon, 291.

37. Grimes, 16.

38. Joan Radner and Susan S. Lanser, "Strategies of Coding in Women's Culture," in Joan Newlon Radner, editor, *Feminist Messages: Coding in Women's Folk Culture* (Urbana: University of Illinois Press, 1993), 1–29.

39. Jane Schaberg, "Response, Special Section on Feminist Translation of the New Testament," *Journal of Feminist Studies in Religion* 6, no. 2 (Fall 1990): 77.

40. Radner and Lanser, 15; see also Annis Pratt, "The New Feminist Criticisms," in Joan Roberts, editor, *Beyond Intellectual Sexism* (New York: David McKay, 1976), 175–95; Melva Wilson Costen, *African American Christian Worship* (Nashville: Abingdon Press, 1993), 36–49.

41. Radner and Lanser, 19.

42. Elaine Lawless, "Writing the Body in the Pulpit: Female-sexed Texts," in *Journal of American Folklore* 107, no. 432 (1994): 55.

43. Elaine Lawless, "Piety and Motherhood: Reproductive Images and Maternal Strategies of the Woman Preacher," in *Journal of American Folklore* 100, no. 398 (1987), 469–78. Similar strategies were also employed by Shaker women who engaged in ecstatic dancing which would have been regarded, even by themselves, as scandalous, if it were not a gift from God. See Marjorie Procter-Smith, *Women in Shaker Community and Worship*, (Lewiston, NY: Edwin Mellen Press, 1985),

44. Joanna Dewey, "Response: Special Section on Feminist Translation of the New Testament, *Journal of Feminist Studies in Religion* vol 6, no. 2 (Fall 1990): 63.

Notes to Chapter Two

1. Catharine MacKinnon, *Toward a Feminist Theory of the State* (Cambridge: Harvard University Press, 1989), 175.

2. Katie Geneva Cannon, *Black Womanist Ethics* (Atlanta: Scholars

Press, 1988); Patricia Hill Collins, *Black Feminist Thought: Knowledge, Consciousness, and the Politics of Empowerment* (New York: Routledge, 1991).

3. *Ibid.*

4. Marge Piercy, "Unlearning not to speak" in *Circles on the Water* (New York: Alfred A. Knopf, Inc., 1971, 1980).

5. Louise Erdrich, "The Veils," in Emilie Buchwald, Pamela R. Fletcher, and Martha Roth, editors, *Transforming a Rape Culture* (Minneapolis: Milkweed Editions, 1993), 338.

6. Sister Mary John Mananzan, editor, *Woman and Religion* (Manila: The Institute of Women's Studies, St. Scholastica's College, 1988), 119. These and the following excerpts are used by permission.

7. Names are pseudonymous in Mananzan's accounts.

8. *The United Methodist Hymnal* (Nashville: United Methodist Publishing House, 1989), 8. My fifteen-year-old son, reading this prayer excerpt aloud over my shoulder, added, in a sarcastic tone, "Spank me! Beat me! I am not worthy!" His gloss recognizes the masochistic tone of the prayer that is spiritualized in the larger context of the liturgy.

9. For a more detailed critique of this and other liturgical elements in light of violence against women, see my article, "'Re-Organizing Victimization': Liturgy and Domestic Violence," in Carol J. Adams and Marie Fortune, editors, *Violence Against Women and Children: A Theological Sourcebook* (New York: Continuum Press, forthcoming). For critique of prayers of confession, see my article, "The Whole Loaf: Holy Communion and Survival," in the same collection.

10. Rebecca Chopp, *The Power to Speak: Feminism, Language, and God* (New York: Crossroad, 1989).

11. Marilyn Frye, *The Politics of Reality: Essays in Feminist Theory* (Freedom, CA: The Crossing Press, 1983), 87.

12. *Ibid.*, 93–94.

13. Beverly Wildung Harrison, *Making the Connections: Essays in Feminist Social Ethics* (Boston: Beacon Press, 1985), 14.

14. On written curses and spells, see John G. Gager, editor, *Curse Tablets and Binding Spells of the Ancient World* (Oxford: Oxford Unversity Press, 1992); Lester K. Little, *Benedictine Maledictions: Liturgical Cursing in Romanesque France* (Ithaca: Cornell University Press, 1993).

15. J. L. Austin, *How to Do Things With Words* (Cambridge, MA: Harvard University Press, 1962).

16. Alice Walker, *The Color Purple* (New York: Harcourt, Brace, Jovanovich, 1982).

17. Kittredge Cherry and Zalmon Sherwood, editors, *Equal Rites: Lesbian and Gay Worship, Ceremonies, and Celebrations.* (Louisville: Westminster/John Knox Press, 1995), 140.

18. For an early example, see Carol Adams, "The Trial of the Hallow-

een Six," in Arlene Swidler, editor, *Sistercelebrations* (Philadelphia: Fortress Press, 1974), 56–67.

19. *The Book of Occasional Services* (New York: Church Hymnal Corporation, 1979), 155.

20. Adrienne Rich, "Natural Resources," *The Dream of a Common Language* (New York: W. W. Norton, 1978), 67.

21. From Daniel J. Harrington, translator, *The Old Testament Pseudepigrapha*, Volume 2, edited by J. H. Charlesworth (Garden City, NY: Doubleday, 1985), 354. As cited in Barbara Bowe, Kathleen Hughes, Sharon Karam, Carolyn Osiek, *Silent Voices, Sacred Lives: Women's Readings for the Liturgical Year* (New York: Paulist Press, 1992), 375.

22. Contemporary prayers and liturgies of lament are found in Frank Henderson, *Liturgies of Lament* (Chicago: Liturgy Training Publications, 1994); David Power, "The Eucharistic Prayer: Another Look," in Frank C. Senn, editor, *New Eucharistic Prayers* (New York: Paulist Press, 1987); David Power, "Forum: Worship After the Holocaust," *Worship* 59, no. 5 (1985).

Notes to Chapter Three

1. Adrienne Rich, *What Is Found There: Notebooks on Poetry and Politics* (New York: W. W. Norton, 1993), 215.

2. Eileen King, "A Lingering Question: What is Feminist Prayer?" in Marjorie Procter-Smith and Janet R. Walton, editors, *Women at Worship: Interpretations of North American Diversity* (Louisville: Westminster/John Knox Press, 1993), 225.

3. Mary Collins, "An Adventuresome Hypothesis: Women as Authors of Liturgical Change," *Proceedings of the North American Academy of Liturgy, 1993*, 46.

4. Lesley A. Northup, "Claiming Horizontal Space: Women's Religious Rituals," *Studia Liturgica* 25 (1995), 92.

5. Rosemary Catalano Mitchell and Gail Anderson Ricciuti, *Birthings and Blessings: Liberating Services for the Inclusive Church* (New York: Crossroad, 1991), 14. Emphasis in original.

6. Northup, 94–98.

7. Gail Anderson Ricciuti and Rosemary Catalano Mitchell, *Birthings and Blessings II: More Liberating Worship Services for the Inclusive Church* (New York: Crossroad, 1993), 32. Emphasis in original.

8. Heilbrun, 37.

9. *Ibid.*, 46.

10. *Ibid.*, 45.

11. Ricciuti and Mitchell, *Birthings and Blessings II*, 31.

12. See Nancy Henley, *Body Politics: Power, Sex, and Nonverbal Communication* (New York: Simon and Schuster, 1977), 36–42; Susan R. Bordo,

"The Body and the Reproduction of Femininity: A Feminist Appropriation of Foucault," in Alison M. Jagger and Susan R. Bordo, editors, *Gender/Body/Knowledge: Feminist Reconstructions of Being and Knowing* (New Brunswick: Rutgers University Press, 1989), 13–33.

13. See Michel Foucault, *Discipline and Punish* (New York: Vintage, 1979), 135–69; Sandra Bartky, "Foucault, Femininity, and the Modernization of Patriarchal Power," in Irene Diamond and Lee Quinby, editors., *Feminism and Foucault: Reflections on Resistance* (Boston: Northeastern University Press, 1988).

14. Margaret Miles, *Carnal Knowing: Female Nakedness and Religious Meaning in the Christian West* (Boston: Beacon Press, 1989), 185.

15. Catharine MacKinnon, *Toward a Feminist Theory of the State*, 179.

16. For a survey of the history of the rite of "churching of women," see Natalie Knodel, "The Thanksgiving of Women after Childbirth, Commonly Called The Churching of Women," unpublished paper.

17. Janet Walton queries, "What about fasting for healing?" I would not regard fasting for healing (either physical or political healing) as self-denial, but as a kind of exorcism. This is clearest, I think, in cases of fasting as protest, but is also true for physical healing.

18. For a valuable examination of the religious meaning of the disabled body, see Nancy Eiesland, *The Disabled God: Toward a Liberatory Theology of Disability* (Nashville: Abingdon Press, 1994).

19. Ursula LeGuin, "'The Author of the Acacia Seeds' and Other Extracts from the Journal of the Association of Therolinguistics," *Buffalo Gals and Other Animal Presences* (New York: Penguin Books, 1987), 210.

20. Charlotte Caron, *To Make and Make Again: Feminist Ritual Thealogy* (New York: Crossroad, 1993), 66.

21. Teal Willoughby, "Ecofeminist Consciousness and the Transforming Power of Symbols," in Carol J. Adams, editor, *Ecofeminism and the Sacred* (New York: Continuum, 1993), 133–35.

22. Rich, 12–13.

23. Audre Lorde, *Sister Outsider: Essays and Speeches* (Freedom, CA: The Crossing Press, 1984), 36.

24. Rich, 85

25. Lorde, 40–41.

26. Text of chant for "Blessing over Milk and Honey," Re-Imagining Conference, November 1993. Used by permission of Reverend Dr. Hilda Kuester.

27. See Johannes Quasten, *Music and Worship in Pagan and Christian Antiquity* (Washington, DC: National Association of Pastoral Musicians, 1983).

28. *Ibid.*, 67–68.

29. Papal Bull of John XXII, *Docta Sanctorum Patrum*, quoted by

Edward Foley in *Music in Ritual: A Pretheological Investigation* (Washington, DC: Pastoral Press, 1984), 4.

30. Quasten, 75–87.

31. Quoted in Foley, 16.

Notes to Chapter Four

1. Margaret Atwood, *Cat's Eye* (New York: Doubleday, 1988), 192.

2. The eucharistic prayer, also called The Great Thanksgiving, is considered in Chapter Six.

3. *The Book of Common Prayer* (New York: Church Hymnal Corporation, 1979), 384. For similar requests, see also the *Book of Common Worship* (Louisville: Westminster/John Knox Press, 1993), 113.

4. See *The Book of Common Prayer*, Form I, 383–85; *The Book of Common Worship*, Prayers of the People G, 118–19.

5. See, for example, William Oddie, *What Will Happen to God? Feminism and the Reconstruction of Christian Belief* (London: SPCK, 1984) and Robert Hamerton-Kelly, *God the Father: Theology and Patriarchy in the Teaching of Jesus* (Philadelphia: Fortress Press, 1979).

6. See, for example, Robert L. Hurd, "Complementarity: A Proposal for Liturgical Language," *Worship* 61, no. 5 (1987): 386–405.

7. *The Book of Common Prayer* 1979 (New York: Church Hymnal Corporation, 1979), 394. The collect cited is a contemporary adaptation of a collect by Thomas Cranmer included in the 1549 Prayer Book.

8. Anne Marie Hunter, "Numbering the Hairs of Our Heads: Male Social Control and the All-Seeing Male God," *Journal of Feminist Studies in Religion* 8, no. 2 (1992): 13.

9. *The Book of Common Worship*, 103.

10. *Ibid.*, 124.

11. Hunter, 24.

12. "Beth's Psalm," in David R. Blumenthal, *Facing the Abusing God: A Theology of Protest* (Louisville: Westminster/John Knox Press, 1993), 229.

13. *Ibid.*, 228.

14. *Ibid.*, 229.

15. *Ibid.*, 247.

16. Joanne Carlson Brown and Rebecca Parker, "For God So Loved the World?" in Joanne Carlson Brown and Carole R. Bohn, editors, *Christianity, Patriarchy and Abuse* (New York: Pilgrim Press, 1989) 16–17.

17. Blumenthal, 197.

18. For a theological consideration of the problem of exploitation of animals in Christian theology, see Carol J. Adams and Marjorie Procter-Smith, "'Taking Life or Taking On Life?' Table Talk and Animals," in Carol J. Adams, editor, *Ecofeminism and the Sacred* (New York: Continuum, 1993).

19. Marilyn Frye, *The Politics of Reality* (Freedom, CA: The Crossing Press, 1983), 82.

20. Blumenthal, 256.

21. Cited in Denise J. J. Dijk, "Developments in Feminist Liturgy in the Netherlands," *Studia Liturgica* 25, no. 1 (1995): 121.

22. The classic statement of this position is that of Carol Christ in "Why Women Need the Goddess," in Carol Christ and Judith Plaskow, editors, *Womanspirit Rising* (San Francisco: Harper and Row, 1979), 273–287 For a Christian argument, see Marjorie Procter-Smith, *In Her Own Rite: Constructing Feminist Liturgical Tradition* (Nashville: Abingdon Press, 1990), Chapter Four.

23. Carol J. Adams, "Toward a Feminist Theology of Religion and the State," in Carol J. Adams and Marie Fortune, editors, *Violence against Women and Children: A Theological Sourcebook* (New York: Continuum Press, forthcoming).

24. Elisabeth Schüssler Fiorenza, *Jesus: Miriam's Child, Sophia's Prophet* (New York: Continuum, 1994), 10.

25. Atwood, 195.

Notes to Chapter Five

1. Kelly Brown Douglas, *The Black Christ* (Maryknoll, NY: Orbis Books, 1994), 177.

2. Paul F. Bradshaw, *Daily Prayer in the Early Church* (New York: Oxford University Press, 1982), 27.

3. *Ibid.*, 30–31.

4. *Ibid.*

5. *Ibid.*, 35–36.

6. *Ibid.*, 36.

7. *Ibid.*, 37.

8. *Ibid.*

9. Elizabeth A. Johnson, *She Who Is: The Mystery of God in Feminist Theological Discourse* (New York: Crossroad, 1992), 151.

10. I examined the general prayers in *The Book of Common Worship*, *The Book of Common Prayer*, *The United Methodist Book of Worship*, and the United Church of Christ *Book of Worship*.

11. Earlier arguments were based on biological and sociological arguments about women's innate weakness.

12. Elisabeth Schüssler Fiorenza, *Jesus: Miriam's Child, Sophia's Prophet* (New York: Continuum Press, 1994), 44.

13. *Ibid.*

14. One of the earliest and perhaps the most familiar of these is Leonard Swidler, "Jesus Was a Feminist," in *Catholic World* 212 (1971), 177–83.

15. Rosemary Radford Ruether, *Sexism and God-Talk: Toward a Feminist Theology* (Boston, Beacon Press, 1983), 137.

16. Rosemary Radford Ruether, "Can Christology be Liberated from Patriarchy?" in *Reconstructing the Christ Symbol: Essays in Feminist Christology,* edited by Maryanne Stevens (New York: Paulist Press, 1993), 23–24.

17. Jacquelyn Grant, "Come to My Help, Lord, for I'm in Trouble," in *Reconstructing the Christ Symbol,* 66–67.

18. Mercy Amba Oduyoye and Elizabeth Amoah, "The Christ for African Women," in Virginia Fabella, M.M., and Mercy Amba Oduyoye, editors, *With Passion and Compassion: Third World Women Doing Theology* (Maryknoll, New York: Orbis Books, 1988), 35–46.

19. *Ibid.,* 38.

20. See Elisabeth Moltmann-Wendell, "Christ in Feminist Context," in Hilary Regan and Alan J. Torrance, editors, *Christ and Context,* (Edinburgh: T & T Clark, 1993) and *The Women Around Jesus* (New York: Crossroad, 1982).

21. Moltmann-Wendell, 110.

22. Rita Nakashima Brock, *Journeys by Heart: A Christology of Erotic Power* (New York: Crossroad, 1988), 52.

23. Carter Heyward, *Speaking of Christ: A Lesbian Feminist Voice* (New York: Pilgrim Press, 1989), 84.

24. See Carolyn Walker Bynum, *Jesus as Mother: Studies in the Spirituality of the High Middle Ages* (Berkeley: University of California Press, 1982).

25. Eleanor McLaughlin, "Feminist Christologies: Re-Dressing the Tradition," in Maryanne Stevens, editor, *Reconstructing the Christ Symbol* (New York: Paulist Press, 1993), 134. See also her "Feminist Christologies: Bodies and Boundaries," in Robert Berkey and Sarah Edwards, editors, *Christology in Dialogue,* (Cleveland, OH: Pilgrim Press, 1993).

26. McLaughlin, 143–44.

27. Johnson, 162.

28. *Ibid.,* 152, 156–57.

29. *Ibid.,* 165.

30. *Ibid.,* 165–66.

31. See Luise Schottroff, *Let the Oppressed Go Free: Feminist Perspectives on the New Testament* (Louisville: Westminster/John Knox Press, 1993).

32. Schüssler Fiorenza, 157.

33. *Ibid.,* 132.

34. *Ibid.,* 162.

35. Odudyoye and Amoah, 42.

36. *Ibid,* 39.

37. Joanne Carlson Brown and Rebecca Parker, "For God So Loved

the World?" in *Christianity, Patriarchy and Abuse: A Feminist Critique*, edited by Joanne Carlson Brown and Carole R. Bohn (New York: Pilgrim Press, 1989), 26.

38. Mary Grey, *Feminism, Redemption, and the Christian Tradition* (London: SCM Press, 1989), 186.

39. Johnson, 159.

40. Chung Hyun Kyung, *Struggle to Be the Sun Again: Introducing Asian Women's Theology* (Maryknoll, NY: Orbis Books, 1990), 71; Kwok Pui-Lan, "God Weeps with Our Pain," *East Asia Journal of Theology* 2, no. 2 (1984): 220–32.

41. Schüssler Fiorenza, 100.

42. *Ibid.*, 111.

43. Carlson Brown and Parker, 2.

44. Millicent C. Feske, "Mistaking Death for Life: Thelma and Louise and Tashi and the Christian Notion of Redemption," unpublished paper, 1.

45. *Ibid.*, 16.

46. *Ibid.*, 17.

47. Carlson Brown and Parker, 28.

48. Delores Williams, "Black Women's Surrogate Experience and the Christian Notion of Redemption," in *After Patriarchy: Feminist Transformation of the World Religions,* edited by Paula M. Cooey, William R. Eakin, and Jay B. McDaniel (Maryknoll, NY: Orbis Books, 1990), 164.

49. *Ibid.*, 165.

50. Oduyoye and Amoah, 39.

51. Virginia Fabella, "A Common Methodology for Diverse Christologies?" in Fabella and Oduyoye, *With Passion and Compassion*, 110.

52. An anonymous Korean woman, quoted in Fabella, "A Common Methodology," 112.

53. Carol J. Adams, *Woman Battering* (Minneapolis: Fortress Press, 1994), 108.

54. *Ibid.*, 109–10.

55. Carlson Brown and Parker, 27.

56. Hoyt L. Hickman, Don E. Saliers, Lawrence Hull Stookey, and James F. White, *The New Handbook of the Christian Year* (Nashville: Abingdon Press, 1986, 1992), 107.

57. The Ministry Unit on Theology and Worship, Presbyterian Church (USA) and the Cumberland Presbyterian Church, *Liturgical Year: The Worship of God* (Louisville: Westminster/John Knox Press, 1992), 35.

58. *Book of Common Prayer,* (New York: Church Hymnal Corporation, 1979), 271; see also *The United Methodist Book of Worship* (Nashville: United Methodist Publishing House, 1992), 340; *The Book of Common Worship*, 253.

59. *Book of Worship: United Church of Christ* (New York: Office for Church Life and Leadership, 1986), 189.

60. *The United Methodist Book of Worship*, 352.

61. *Ibid.*, 372.

62. Janet Morley, *All Desires Known: Inclusive Prayers for Worship and Meditation* (Harrisburg, PA: Morehouse Publishing, 1988, 1992), 9.

63. Miriam Therese Winter, Adair Lummis, and Allison Stokes, *Defecting in Place: Women Claiming Responsibility for Their Own Spiritual Lives* (New York: Crossroad, 1994), 183.

64. *Ibid.*, 161.

65. Rosemary Catalano Mitchell and Gail Anderson Ricciuti, *Birthings and Blessings: Liberating Worship Services for the Inclusive Church* (New York: Crossroad, 1991); see also Mitchell and Ricciuti, *Birthings and Blessings II* (New York: Crossroad, 1993).

66. Diann Neu, "Women-Church Transforming Liturgy," in *Women at Worship: Interpretations of North American Diversity*, edited by Marjorie Procter-Smith and Janet R. Walton (Louisville: Westminster/John Knox Press, 1993), 164. For the full text of the liturgy, see Diann L. Neu and Mary E. Hunt, *Women of Fire: A Pentecost Event* (Silver Spring, MD: WATERworks Press, 1990).

67. See, for example, the hymn "Fairest Sophia," a rewritten version of the hymn "Fairest Lord Jesus," in Susan Cady, Marian Ronan, and Hal Taussig, *Wisdom's Feast: Sophia in Study and Celebration* (San Francisco: Harper & Row, 1989), 185.

68. *Ibid.*, 66.

69. *Ibid.*, 119.

70. *Ibid.*

71. See for example, Tom Oden, "Encountering the Goddess at Church," *Good News* (November-December 1993): 42.

72. Chung Hyun Kyung, *Struggle to Be the Sun Again*, 73 and Heather Murray Elkins' discussion of controversy over Sophia in her book, *Worshiping Women: Re-Forming God's People for Praise* (Nashville: Abingdon Press, 1994), 167–70.

73. See, for example, Carol J. Adams and Marjorie Procter-Smith, "Taking Life or 'Taking On Life'? Table Talk and Animals," in *Ecofeminism and the Sacred*, Carol J. Adams, editor (New York: Continuum, 1993), 295–310. See also Carol J. Adams, *Neither Man nor Beast: Feminism and the Defense of Animals* (New York: Continuum, 1994); Andrew Linzey, *Christianity and the Rights of Animals* (New York: Crossroad, 1987) and *Animal Theology* (London: SCM Press, 1994); Tom Regan, *The Thee Generation: Reflections on the Coming Revolution* (Philadelphia: Temple University Press, 1991).

Notes to Chapter Six

1. Elisabeth Schüssler Fiorenza, *In Memory of Her* (New York: Crossroad, 1983), 350.

2. Miriam Therese Winter, Adair Lummis, and Allison Stokes, *Defecting in Place: Women Claiming Responsibility for Their Own Spiritual Lives* (New York: Crossroad, 1994), 84.

3. *Ibid.*, 86.

4. *Ibid.*, 115.

5. *Ibid.*, 73.

6. For further development of these issues see my article, "The Whole Loaf: Holy Communion and Survival," in Carol J. Adams and Marie Fortune, editors, *Violence against Women and Children: A Christian Theological Sourcebook* (New York: Continuum, forthcoming), 489–503.

7. Rafael Avila, *Worship and Politics* (Maryknoll, NY: Orbis Books, 1981), 100, 105.

8. Arlo Duba, "Presbyterian Eucharistic Prayers," in Frank C. Senn, editor, *New Eucharistic Prayers: An Ecumenical Study of Their Development and Structure* (New York: Paulist Press, 1987), 99.

9. *Ibid.*, 101; Prayer B in the *Book of Common Worship* (Louisville: Westminster/John Knox Press, 1993)

10. *Commentary on Prayer Book Studies 30, Containing Supplemental Liturgical Texts* (New York: Church Hymnal Corporation, 1989), C-15.

11. *Ibid.*, 66–73.

12. Itumeleng Mosala, *Biblical Hermeneutics and Black Theology in South Africa* (Grand Rapids, MI: Eerdmans Press, 1989).

13. The literature on this is vast. For example, see Joachim Jeremias, *The Eucharistic Words of Jesus* (London: SCM Press, 1966); Hans Schurmann, "Jesus' Words in the Light of his Actions at the Last Supper," in Pierre Benoit, editor, *Concilium* 40 (New York: Paulist Press, 1969); William R. Crockett, *Eucharist: Symbol of Transformation* (New York: Pueblo Press, 1989); Jean-Jacques von Allman, *The Lord's Supper* (London: Lutterworth Press, 1969).

14. Crockett, 63.

15. Joanna Dewey, "Sacrifice, the Bible and Christ," in Letty Russell, editor, *A Dictionary of Feminist Theologies* (Louisville: Westminster/John Knox, forthcoming).

16. *Didache* 14:1–3

17. Faith and Order Paper No. 111, *Baptism, Eucharist and Ministry* (Geneva: WCC, 1982), 11.

18. Nancy Jay, *Throughout Your Generations Forever: Sacrifice, Religion, and Paternity* (Chicago: University Of Chicago Press, 1992), 147.

19. *Ibid.*, 116.

20. *Ibid.*, 114–15.

21. *Ibid.*, 121–25.

22. *The United Methodist Hymnal* (Nashville: United Methodist Publishing House, 1989), 616.

23. *Ibid.*, 369.

24. *Ibid.*, 622.

25. *Ibid.*, 370.

26. Gordon Lathrop, *Holy Things: A Liturgical Theology* (Minneapolis: Fortress Press, 1993), 141.

27. *Ibid.*, 155.

28. Gail Ramshaw-Schmidt, "Toward Lutheran Eucharistic Prayers," in Senn, 77–78.

29. Jay, 148.

30. For a comparative review of contemporary reforms, see Senn; see also Max Thurian and Geoffrey Wainwright, *Baptism and Eucharist: Ecumenical Convergence in Celebration* (Geneva: WCC, 1983).

31. See Dennis E. Smith and Hal Taussig, *Many Tables: The Eucharist in the New Testament and the Liturgy Today* (Philadelphia: Trinity Press International, London: SCM Press, 1990).

32. Arlo Duba, "Presbyterian Eucharistic Prayers," in Senn, 106.

33. David Power, "The Eucharistic Prayer: Another Look," in Senn, 249.

34. *Ibid.*, 248.

35. Sheila Redmond, "Christian 'Virtues' and Child Sexual Abuse," in Joanne Carlson Brown and Rebecca Parker, *Christianity, Patriarchy and Abuse: A Feminist Critique* (New York: Pilgrim Press, 1989), 70–88.

36. Ritual prepared and led by Nan Liliane Hofheinz and Peggy Cheney.

37. For examples of liturgies patterned after the psalms of lament, see Frank Henderson, *Liturgies of Lament* (Chicago: Liturgy Training Publications, 1994).

38. Prepared for Women's Week, Perkins School of Theology, 1991.

39. This phrase suggested by Millicent C. Feske.

Notes to Epilogue

1. For a working list of such criteria, developed from work with feminist liturgy and ritual groups, see my summary of discussion of the Feminist Liturgy Seminar of the North American Academy of Liturgy, "The Marks of Feminist Liturgy," *Proceedings of the North American Academy of Liturgy*, 1992.

2. Alice Walker, *In Search of Our Mothers' Gardens* (San Diego: Harcourt, Brace, Jovanovich, 1983), xi.

Collections of Feminist Prayers and Liturgies

Bowe, Barbara, Kathleen Hughes, Sharon Karam, and Carolyn Osiek. *Silent Voices, Sacred Lives: Women's Readings for the Liturgical Year.* New York: Paulist Press, 1992.

Cady, Susan, Hal Taussig, and Marian Ronan. *Wisdom's Feast: Sophia in Study and Celebration.* San Francisco: Harper and Row, 1989.

Cherry, Kittredge and Zalmon Sherwood, editors. *Equal Rites: Lesbian and Gay Worship, Ceremonies, and Celebrations.* Louisville: Westminster/ John Knox Press, 1995.

Kirk, Martha Ann. *Celebrations of Biblical Women's Stories: Tears, Milk and Honey.* Kansas City, MO: Sheed and Ward, 1987.

Mitchell, Rosemary Catalano and Gail Anderson Ricciuti. *Birthings and Blessings II: More Liberating Worship Services for the Inclusive Church.* New York: Crossroad, 1993.

———. *Birthings and Blessings: Liberating Services for the Inclusive Church.* New York: Crossroad, 1991.

Morley, Janet. *All Desires Known: Inclusive Prayers for Worship and Meditation.* Harrisburg, PA: Morehouse Publishing, 1988, 1992.

Neu, Diann L. *Women and the Gospel Traditions: Feminist Celebrations.* Silver Spring, MD: WATERworks Press, 1989.

———. *WomenChurch Celebrations: Feminist Liturgies for the Lenten Season.* Silver Spring, MD: WATER Resources, 1985.

Neu, Diann L. and Mary E. Hunt. *Women of Fire: a Pentecost Event.* Silver Spring, MD: WATERworks Press, 1990.

Schmitt, Mary Kathleen Speegle. *Seasons of the Feminine Divine: Christian Feminist Prayers for the Liturgical Cycle.* New York: Crossroad, 1993.

St. Hilda Community. *Women Included: A Book of Services and Prayers.* London: SPCK, 1991.

Swidler, Arlene, editor. *Sistercelebrations.* Philadelphia: Fortress Press, 1974.

Winter, Miriam Therese. *WomanPrayer, WomanSong: Resources for Ritual.* Oak Park, Illinois: Meyer Stone Books, 1987.

———. *WomanWisdom: A Feminist Lectionary and Psalter. Women of the Hebrew Scriptures: Part One.* New York: Crossroad, 1991.

———. *WomanWitness: A Feminist Lectionary and Psalter. Women of the Hebrew Scriptures: Part Two.* New York: Crossroad, 1992.

———. *WomanWord: A Feminist Lectionary and Psalter. Women of the New Testament*. New York: Crossroad, 1990.

Other Works of Interest

Adams, Carol J. *Neither Man nor Beast: Feminism and the Defense of Animals*. New York: Continuum, 1994.

———. "Toward a Feminist Theology of Religion and the State." In *Violence against Women and Children: A Theological Sourcebook*, edited by Carol J. Adams and Marie Fortune. New York: Continuum Press, forthcoming.

———. *Woman Battering*. Minneapolis: Fortress Press, 1994.

———, editor. *Ecofeminism and the Sacred*. New York: Continuum, 1993.

Adams, Carol J. and Marjorie Procter-Smith. "'Taking Life or Taking On Life?' Table Talk and Animals." In *Ecofeminism and the Sacred*, edited by Carol J. Adams. New York: Continuum, 1993.

Avila, Rafael. *Worship and Politics*. Maryknoll, NY: Orbis Books, 1981.

Blumenthal, David R. *Facing the Abusing God: A Theology of Protest*. Louisville: Westminster/John Knox Press, 1993.

Bradshaw, Paul F. *Daily Prayer in the Early Church*. New York: Oxford University Press, 1982.

Brock, Rita Nakashima. *Journeys by Heart: A Christology of Erotic Power*. New York: Crossroad, 1988.

Buchwald, Emilie, Pamela R. Fletcher, and Martha Roth, editors. *Transforming a Rape Culture*. Minneapolis: Milkweed Editions, 1993.

Bynum, Carolyn Walker. *Jesus as Mother: Studies in the Spirituality of the High Middle Ages*. Berkeley: University of California Press, 1982.

Cannon, Katie Geneva. *Black Womanist Ethics*. Atlanta: Scholars Press, 1988.

Carlson Brown, Joanne and Carole R. Bohn, editors. *Christianity, Patriarchy and Abuse*. New York: Pilgrim Press, 1989.

Carlson Brown, Joanne and Rebecca Parker. "For God So Loved the World?" In *Christianity, Patriarchy and Abuse*, edited by Joanne Carlson Brown and Carole R. Bohn. New York: Pilgrim Press, 1989.

Caron, Charlotte. *To Make and Make Again: Feminist Ritual Thealogy*. New York: Crossroad, 1993.

Chopp, Rebecca. *The Power to Speak: Feminism, Language, and God*. New York: Crossroad, 1989.

Christ, Carol. "Why Women Need the Goddess." In *Womanspirit Rising*, edited by Carol Christ and Judith Plaskow. San Francisco: Harper and Row, 1979.

Chung Hyun Kyung, *Struggle to Be the Sun Again: Introducing Asian Women's Theology*. Maryknoll, NY: Orbis Books, 1990.

Collins, Mary. "An Adventuresome Hypothesis: Women as Authors of

Liturgical Change." *Proceedings of the North American Academy of Liturgy, 1993.*

Collins, Patricia Hill. *Black Feminist Thought: Knowledge, Consciousness, and the Politics of Empowerment.* New York: Routledge, 1991.

Dewey, Joanna. "Response: Special Section on Feminist Translation of the New Testament," *Journal of Feminist Studies in Religion* vol 6, no. 2 (Fall 1990).

————. "Sacrifice, the Bible and Christ." In *A Dictionary of Feminist Theologies,* edited by Letty Russell. New York: Crossroad, forthcoming.

Diamond, Irene and Lee Quinby, editors. *Feminism and Foucault: Reflections on Resistance.* Boston: Northeastern University Press, 1988.

Dijk, Denise J. J. "Developments in Feminist Liturgy in the Netherlands." *Studia Liturgica* 25, no. 1 (1995).

Duba, Arlo. "Presbyterian Eucharistic Prayers." In *New Eucharistic Prayers: An Ecumenical Study of Their Development and Structure,* edited by Frank C. Senn. New York: Paulist Press, 1987.

Eiesland, Nancy. *The Disabled God: Toward a Liberatory Theology of Disability.* Nashville: Abingdon Press, 1994.

Elkins, Heather Murray. *Worshiping Women: Re-Forming God's People for Praise.* Nashville: Abingdon Press, 1994.

Fabella, Virginia. "A Common Methodology for Diverse Christologies?" In *With Passion and Compassion: Third World Women Doing Theology,* edited by Fabella and Oduyoye, editors. Maryknoll, NY: Orbis Books, 1988.

Fabella, Virginia and Mercy Amba Oduyoye, editors. *With Passion and Compassion: Third World Women Doing Theology.* Maryknoll, NY: Orbis Books, 1988.

Frye, Marilyn. *The Politics of Reality: Essays in Feminist Theory.* Freedom, CA: The Crossing Press, 1983.

Grant, Jacquelyn. "Come to My Help, Lord, for I'm in Trouble." In *Reconstructing the Christ Symbol,* edited by Maryanne Stevens. New York: Paulist Press, 1993.

Grey, Mary. *Feminism, Redemption, and the Christian Tradition.* London: SCM Press, 1989.

Grimes, Ronald. *Reading, Writing, and Ritualizing.* Washington, DC: The Pastoral Press, 1993.

Harrison, Beverly Wildung. *Making the Connections: Essays in Feminist Social Ethics.* Boston: Beacon Press, 1985.

Heilbrun, Carolyn. *Writing a Woman's Life.* New York: Ballantine Books, 1988.

Henley, Nancy. *Body Politics: Power, Sex, and Nonverbal Communication.* New York: Simon and Schuster, 1977.

Heyward, Carter. *Speaking of Christ: A Lesbian Feminist Voice.* New York: Pilgrim Press, 1989.

hooks, bell. *Teaching to Transgress: Education as the Practice of Freedom*. New York: Routledge, 1994.

Hunter, Anne Marie. "Numbering the Hairs of Our Heads: Male Social Control and the All-Seeing Male God." *Journal of Feminist Studies in Religion* 8, no. 2 (1992).

Jagger, Alison M. and Susan R. Bordon, editors. *Gender/Body/Knowledge: Feminist Reconstructions of Being and Knowing*. New Brunswick: Rutgers University Press, 1989.

Jay, Nancy. "Gender and Dichotomy," *Feminist Studies* 7, no. 1 (1981).

———. *Throughout Your Generations Forever: Sacrifice, Religion, and Paternity*. Chicago: University of Chicago Press, 1992.

Johnson, Elizabeth A. *She Who Is: The Mystery of God in Feminist Theological Discourse*. New York: Crossroad, 1992.

Kwok Pui-Lan, "God Weeps with Our Pain," *East Asia Journal of Theology* 2, no. 2 (1984).

Lathrop, Gordon. *Holy Things: A Liturgical Theology*. Minneapolis: Fortress Press, 1993.

Lawless, Elaine. "Piety and Motherhood: Reproductive Images and Maternal Strategies of the Woman Preacher." *Journal of American Folklore* 100, no. 398 (1987).

———. "Writing the Body in the Pulpit: Female-Sexed Texts." *Journal of American Folklore* 107, no. 432 (1994).

Lorde, Audre. *Sister Outsider: Essays and Speeches*. Freedom, CA: The Crossing Press, 1984.

MacKinnon, Catharine. *Toward a Feminist Theory of the State*. Cambridge, MA: Harvard University Press, 1989.

Mananzan, Sister Mary John, editor. *Woman and Religion*. Manila: The Institute of Women's Studies, St. Scholastica's College, 1988.

McLaughlin, Eleanor. "Feminist Christologies: Bodies and Boundaries." In *Christology in Dialogue*, edited by Robert Berkey and Sarah Edwards. Cleveland, OH: Pilgrim Press, 1993.

———. "Feminist Christologies: Re-Dressing the Tradition." In *Reconstructing the Christ Symbol*, edited by Maryanne Stevens. New York: Paulist Press, 1993.

Miles, Margaret. *Carnal Knowing: Female Nakedness and Religious Meaning in the Christian West*. Boston: Beacon Press, 1989.

Moltmann-Wendell, Elisabeth. "Christ in Feminist Context." In *Christ and Context*, edited by Hilary Regan and Alan J. Torrance. Edinburgh: T & T Clark, 1993.

———. *The Women Around Jesus*. New York: Crossroad, 1982.

Mosala, Itumeleng. *Biblical Hermeneutics and Black Theology in South Africa*. Grand Rapids, MI: Eerdmans Press, 1989.

Norén, Carol. *Woman in the Pulpit*. Nashville: Abingdon Press, 1991.

Northup, Lesley A. "Claiming Horizontal Religious Space: Women's Religious Rituals." *Studia Liturgica* 25, no. 1 (1995).

———, editor. *Women and Religious Ritual.* Washington, DC: The Pastoral Press, 1993.

Oduyoye, Mercy Amba and Elizabeth Amoah. "The Christ for African Women." In *With Passion and Compassion: Third World Women Doing Theology,* edited by Virginia Fabella, M.M., and Mercy Amba Oduyoye. Maryknoll, NY: Orbis Books, 1988.

Power, David N., O.M.I. "The Anamnesis: Remembering, We Offer." In *New Eucharistic Prayers: An Ecumenical Study of Their Development and Structure,* edited by Frank C. Senn. New York: Paulist Press, 1987.

———. "The Eucharistic Prayer: Another Look." In *New Eucharistic Prayers: An Ecumenical Study of Their Development and Structure,* edited by Frank C. Senn. New York: Paulist Press, 1987.

Procter-Smith, Marjorie and Janet Walton, editors. *Women at Worship: Interpretations of North American Diversity.* Louisville: Westminster/ John Knox, 1994.

Procter-Smith, Marjorie. "'Re-Organizing Victimization': Liturgy and Domestic Violence." In *Violence Against Women and Children: A Theological Sourcebook,* edited by Carol J. Adams and Marie Fortune. New York: Continuum Press, forthcoming.

———. *In Her Own Rite: Constructing Feminist Liturgical Tradition.* Nashville: Abingdon Press, 1990.

———. "The Marks of Feminist Liturgy," *Proceedings of the North American Academy of Liturgy, 1992.*

———. "The Whole Loaf: Holy Communion and Survival." In *Violence Against Women and Children: A Theological Sourcebook,* edited by Carol J. Adams and Marie Fortune. New York: Continuum Press, forthcoming.

Radford Ruether, Rosemary. "Can Christology be Liberated from Patriarchy?" In *Reconstructing the Christ Symbol: Essays in Feminist Christology,* edited by Maryanne Stevens. New York: Paulist Press, 1993.

———. *Sexism and God-Talk: Toward a Feminist Theology.* Boston: Beacon Press, 1983.

Radner, Joan Newlon, editor. *Feminist Messages: Coding in Women's Folk Culture.* Urbana: University of Illinois Press, 1993.

Ramshaw-Schmidt, Gail. "Toward Lutheran Eucharistic Prayers." In *New Eucharistic Prayers: An Ecumenical Study of Their Development and Structure,* edited by Frank C. Senn, editor. New York: Paulist Press, 1987.

Raymond, Janice. *A Passion For Friends: Toward a Philosophy of Female Affection.* Boston: Beacon Press, 1986.

Redmond, Sheila. "Christian 'Virtues' and Child Sexual Abuse." In *Chris-*

tianity, Patriarchy and Abuse: a Feminist Critique, edited by Joanne Carlson Brown and Rebecca Parker. New York: Pilgrim Press, 1989.

Rich, Adrienne. *What is Found There: Notebooks on Poetry and Politics.* New York: W. W. Norton, 1993.

Schaberg, Jane. "Response, Special Section on Feminist Translation of the New Testament." *Journal of Feminist Studies in Religion* 6, no. 2 (Fall 1990).

Schottroff, Luise. *Let the Oppressed Go Free: Feminist Perspectives on the New Testament.* Louisville: Westminster/John Knox Press, 1993.

Schüssler Fiorenza, Elisabeth. *But She Said: Feminist Practices of Biblical Interpretation.* Boston: Beacon Press, 1992.

———. *Jesus: Miriam's Child, Sophia's Prophet: Critical Issues in Feminist Christology.* New York: Continuum, 1994.

Senn, Frank C., editor. *New Eucharistic Prayers: An Ecumenical Study of Their Development and Structure.* New York: Paulist Press, 1987.

Smith, Christine M. *Preaching as Weeping, Confession, and Resistance: Radical Responses to Radical Evil.* Louisville: Westminster/John Knox Press, 1992.

———. *Weaving the Sermon: Preaching in a Feminist Perspective.* Louisville: Westminster/John Knox Press, 1989.

Smith, Dennis E. and Hal Taussig. *Many Tables: The Eucharist in the New Testament and the Liturgy Today.* Philadelphia: Trinity Press International, London: SCM Press, 1990.

Stevens, Maryanne, editor. *Reconstructing the Christ Symbol.* New York: Paulist Press, 1993.

Thurian, Max and Geoffrey Wainwright. *Baptism and Eucharist: Ecumenical Convergence in Celebration.* Geneva: WCC, 1983.

Walton, Janet. "Ecclesial and Feminist Blessing: Women as Objects and Subjects of the Power of Blessing." In *Blessing and Power,* edited by Mary Collins and David Power. Edinburgh: T & T Clark, 1985.

Williams, Delores. "Black Women's Surrogate Experience and the Christian Notion of Redemption." In *After Patriarchy: Feminist Transformation of the World Religions,* edited by Paula M. Cooey, William R. Eakin, and Jay B. McDaniel. Maryknoll, NY: Orbis Books, 1990.

Willoughby, L. Teal. "Ecofeminist Consciousness and the Transforming Power of Symbols." In *Ecofeminist and the Sacred,* edited by Carol J. Adams. New York: Continuum, 1993.

Winter, Miriam Therese, Adair Lummis, and Alison Stokes. *Defecting in Place: Women Claiming Responsibility for Their Own Spiritual Lives.* New York: Crossroad Press, 1994.